Buckle Down®

to the
Common Core
State Standards

English Language Arts

Grade 4

This book belongs to: _____

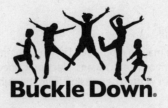

Buckle Down™

Helping your schoolhouse meet the standards of the statehouse™

Acknowledgment

Every effort has been made by the publisher to locate each owner of the copyrighted material reprinted in this publication and to secure the necessary permissions. If there are any questions regarding the use of these materials, the publisher will take appropriate corrective measures to acknowledge ownership in future publications.

ISBN 978-0-7836-8050-7

1CCUS04RD01   7 8 9 10

Contributing Writer: John Ham
Cover Image: Winding road through the forest in the Appalachian Mountains. © Alexey Stiop/Dreamstime.com

Triumph Learning® 136 Madison Avenue, 7th Floor, New York, NY 10016

Frequently Asked Questions about the Common Core State Standards

What are the Common Core State Standards?

The Common Core State Standards for English Language Arts, grades K–12, are a set of shared goals and expectations for what knowledge and skills will help students succeed. They allow students to understand what is expected of them and to become progressively more proficient in understanding and using English Language Arts. At the same time, teachers will be better equipped to know exactly what they need to help students learn and establish individualized benchmarks for them.

Will the Common Core State Standards tell teachers how and what to teach?

No. The best understanding of what works in the classroom comes from the teachers who are in them. That's why these standards will establish *what* students need to learn, but they will not dictate *how* teachers should teach. Instead, schools and teachers will decide how best to help students reach the standards.

What will the Common Core State Standards mean for students?

The standards will provide more clarity about and consistency in what is expected of student learning across the country. Common standards will not prevent different levels of achievement among students, but they will ensure more consistent exposure to materials and learning experiences through curriculum, instruction, and teacher preparation among other supports for student learning. These standards will help prepare students with the knowledge and skills they need to succeed in college and careers.

Do the Common Core State Standards focus on skills and content knowledge?

Yes. The Common Core State Standards recognize that both content and skills are important. The Common Core State Standards contain rigorous content and application of knowledge through high-order thinking skills. The English Language Arts standards require certain critical content for all students, including: classic myths and stories from around the world, America's founding documents, foundational American literature, and Shakespeare. The remaining crucial decisions about what content should be taught are left to state and local determination. In addition to content coverage, the Common Core State Standards require that students systematically acquire knowledge in literature and other disciplines through reading, writing, speaking, and listening.

The Common Core State Standards also require that students develop a depth of understanding and ability to apply English Language Arts to novel situations, as college students and employees regularly do.

Will common assessments be developed? When will they be ready?

It will be up to the states: some states plan to come together voluntarily to develop a common assessment system. A state-led consortium on assessment would be grounded in the following principles: allow for comparison across students, schools, districts, states, and nations; create economies of scale; provide information and support more effective teaching and learning; and prepare students for college and careers.

A common assessment could be in place in some states by the 2014–2015 school year.

TABLE OF CONTENTS

To the Teacher:

Common Core State Standards are listed for each lesson in the table of contents and for each page in the shaded gray bars that run across the tops of the pages in the workbook (see the example at right).

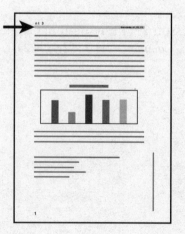

Reading

You read all the time, for many reasons. At school, you read to learn about math, science, and the arts. At home, you read to find out how to play games, what time movies start, and when your favorite band will put out a new CD. By now, you're a better reader than you know.

In this unit, you will work on becoming an even *better* reader. You will learn some ways of figuring out new words. You will practice telling what a story is mostly about. Then, you will begin to dig a little deeper.

This unit will help you see how one idea links to another. You will think about the way stories work. You will notice how pieces of writing are alike and different. You will learn some of the ways authors make their writing interesting. You will find out how they put their ideas in order.

By the time you finish the lessons in this unit, you will be a better reader than ever.

In This Unit

Word Parts

Word Meaning

Main Idea and Details

Getting the Most from What You Read

Poetry, Prose, and Drama

Story Elements

Literary Devices

Informational Text

Text Structures

Information You Can See

Comparing Passages

CCS: L.4.4b

Lesson 1: Word Parts

Words are not like flowers. You can't sprinkle water over them and watch them grow into larger words. Instead, you can learn how small words grow into large words by learning about prefixes, suffixes, and root words. You can also learn a lot about making and growing words by learning where these words come from.

Prefixes, Suffixes, and Root Words

Many words in the English language are made up of smaller word parts. These parts include root words and affixes. A **root word** is the basic part of a word. Root words mostly come from Latin and Greek. For example, *graph* is the root word of *graphic*. **Affixes** are the letters added to the beginning or end of a root word. These letters change the word's meaning. They may change the meaning a little or a lot. Prefixes and suffixes are the two types of affixes. Learning some common prefixes and suffixes will help you understand more of what you read.

 TIP 1: Prefixes go before root words.

A **prefix** is a word part added to the beginning of a root word. Adding a prefix to a root word is like adding a link to a chain. The prefix and word simply hook together.

When you add a prefix to a root word, the meaning of the word changes. For example, *unhappy* does not mean the same thing as *happy*.

CCS: L.4.4b

The following table shows some common prefixes and their meanings.

Prefix	Meaning	Example
dis-	the opposite of, not	discover displace
im-	not	impolite improper
in-	not	indefinite incorrect
mis-	badly, wrong, not	mismanage misspell
multi-	many	multipurpose multivitamin
non-	not, the opposite of	nonliving nonsense
over-	beyond, more than	overcook overwork
pre-	before	pregame preheat
re-	again	reconnect redraw
un-	the opposite of, not	unfriendly unpleasant
under-	beneath, less than	undersea underfoot

Fill in the following table to see how prefixes can change the meanings of root words. Use the prefix table to help you.

Affixed Word	Prefix	Root Word	Meaning of Affixed Word
distrust	dis-	trust	not having trust
impatient			not patient
invisible	in-		
mistake		take	
multicolor			having many colors
nonfat	non-		
overdone		done	
prewriting			before writing (planning)
reuse	re-		
untrue		true	
underline			line beneath something

The next activity will help you practice making your own words using prefixes.

CCS: L.4.4b

Practice Activity 1

Directions: Add a root word to each prefix. Next to each example, write the meaning of the new word. Use a dictionary for help if you need it. The first one has been done for you.

1. dis-   *disrespect: not having respect* _____

2. im-   _____

3. in-   _____

4. mis-   _____

5. multi-   _____

6. non-   _____

7. over-   _____

8. pre-   _____

9. re-   _____

10. un-   _____

11. under-   _____

TIP 2: Suffixes go after root words.

A **suffix** is a word part added to the end of a root word. Adding a suffix changes the meaning of the root word. Think about the word *happy* again. If you add the suffix *-ness*, you make the word *happiness*. You can't always just stick a suffix on a root word. Sometimes, you must change the spelling of the root in the new word. Notice that when we added the suffix *–ness* to *happy,* we dropped the *y* and changed it to an *i*.

The following table shows some common suffixes and their meanings.

Suffix	Meaning	Example
-able	able to be or become something worthy of being or becoming something	acceptable washable
-en	to make or become made from	lighten wooden
-er, -or	person who	baker inventor
-ful	acting in a certain way having a lot of something	thankful healthful
-ish	belonging to a nation like somewhat	Swedish selfish bluish
-less	without missing something	waterless sleepless
-ly	in such a way as happening sometimes	gently daily
-ment	action or process result of action or process	government measurement
-ness	a way of being something appearing some way	tenderness redness
-ous	full of having	joyous famous
-y	full of having a lot of something	scary drippy

CCS: L.4.4b

Fill in the following table to see how suffixes can change the meanings of root words. Use the suffix table to help you.

Affixed Word	Root Word	Suffix	Meaning of Affixed Word
straighten	straight	-en	to make straight
helpful	help		
breakable		-able	
coldish			somewhat cold
mindless	mind		
slowly		-ly	
payment			act of paying
kindness	kind		
decorator		-or	
wondrous			full of wonder
bubbly	bubble		

The next activity will help you practice making your own words using suffixes.

Practice Activity 2

Directions: Add a root word to each suffix. Next to each example, write the meaning of the new word. Use a dictionary for help if you need it. The first one has been done for you.

1. -able   *admirable: able to be admired* _____

2. -er or -or _____

3. -ful   _____

4. -ish   _____

5. -less   _____

6. -ly   _____

7. -ment   _____

8. -ness   _____

9. -en   _____

10. -ous   _____

11. -y   _____

TIP 3: Both prefixes and suffixes can be added to root words.

A root word can have both a prefix and a suffix added to it. Some even have more than one of each. Here are a couple of examples. Fill in the blank spaces in the table.

Prefix +	Root Word	+ Suffix	Affixed Word	Meaning of Affixed Word
un-		-able	unusable	
mis-		-ment	mismanagement	

Practice Activity 3

Directions: Write the meaning of each word on the line provided. Use the prefix table on page 9 to help you. The first one has been done for you.

1. rewrite

   _write again_____

2. impossible

   _____

3. unknowable

   _____

4. misunderstood

   _____

5. pregame

   _____

Write a word using a suffix that means the same as each of the following groups of words. Use the suffix table on page 12 to help you. The first one has been done for you.

6. able to be washed

   washable

7. make short

8. full of thanks

9. a way of being clever

 TIP 4: Root words can help you figure out new words.

Knowing the meanings of common root words can help you figure out new words. Here are some common root words you should know.

Root Word	Meaning	Example
aqua	water	aquarium, aquatic
dict	say	dictionary, predict
loc	place	locate, location
micro	small	microscope, microwave
port	carry	portable, transport
struct	build	construct, structure
therm	heat	thermometer, thermos
tract	pull	attract, tractor
zo	animal	zoo, zoology

CCS: L.4.4b

Practice Activity 4

Directions: Write the meaning of each word on the line provided. Use the root word table to help you. You may also use a dictionary if you need it. The first one has been done for you.

1. dictate

   to say or read out loud

2. local

   _____

3. zookeeper

   _____

4. support

   _____

5. instruct

   _____

6. microcomputer

   _____

Word Sounds

We get much more practice with speaking and listening than with reading. Often, words on a page will make more sense if you hear them.

 TIP 5: Sound out unknown words to figure out their meaning.

When you see an unknown word, try sounding out the word. Use what you know about letter sounds to figure out how the word is pronounced. If you're taking a reading test, sound out the word in your head, not out loud. Listen for word parts (prefixes, root words, and suffixes) you already know. Or listen for smaller words within the larger word. If you can sound out a difficult word, you may be able to figure out what it means.

 TIP 6: Use what you know about word sounds to figure out new words and how to pronounce them.

Here is a quick review about sounding out words.

- The letters *c* and *g* can make a hard sound or a soft sound.

Hard	Soft
castle	citizen
gravy	general

- The letter *k* can make a hard sound or remain silent.

Hard	Silent
kingdom	knee

- Words can say their sounds in letter order or blend their sounds. Sometimes, two or more letters can make a new sound. Here are some examples:

In order:	cat (c + a + t)	mop (m + o + p)	deep (d + e + e + p)
Blend:	black	truck	flew
New sound:	shoe	think	tough

- Most of the time, when a vowel is followed by one or more consonants (except *r*), it has a short-vowel sound.

  l**i**p   l**i**d   s**u**n   **a**pple   m**o**p   **a**t   **i**t   g**e**t

- Most of the time, when a vowel is followed by a consonant and a final *e*, it has a long vowel sound and the *e* is silent.

  br**a**ve   s**i**de   t**u**ne   h**o**me   sch**e**me

- Most of the time, when a vowel is followed by two or more consonants and a final *e*, it has a short vowel sound and the *e* is silent.

  pr**a**nce   d**e**nse   br**i**dge   l**o**dge   pl**u**nge

- Usually, when two vowels are side-by-side in a word, the first vowel has a long sound and the second vowel is silent.

  t**oa**st   s**ea**side   b**ai**t   t**oe**   j**ui**ce

- A single vowel at the end of a word often has a long vowel sound.

  h**e**   g**o**   h**i**   sh**e**   n**o**   b**e**   fl**u**

TIP 7: Use word sounds to figure out how to say words that look alike.

Words often look alike but sound different. For example, the word *dinner* has one more *n* than *diner*. But that *n* makes all the difference in how it sounds. The second *n* in *dinner* makes the *i* sound like the *i* in *pin*. The same is true about the words *robe* and *robber*. The word *robe* follows the silent-*e* rule you learned about in Tip 6. But the second *b* in *robber* makes the *o* sound like the *o* in *job*.

When you find words that look like other words, do your best to remember the rules and sound them out.

Lesson Practice begins on the following page.

Directions: This passage is about a boy who has to walk home in the dark. Read the passage. Then answer Numbers 1 through 8.

from

Fright in the Forest

by Kay Kryptson

"If we played one more game, I could beat you," Scott said. He and his cousin Bridgette had been playing Chinese checkers for three hours straight. Bridgette had been successful every time. "But I've got to get home or Mom's gonna have a cow."

"Yeah, you were supposed to be home an hour ago," Bridgette said. "Now you'll have to walk in the dark—without a flashlight."

Scott and Bridgette lived on opposite sides of a small wooded area. Picken's Forest, it was called. Scott didn't think it was big enough to be called a forest. The trees certainly were thick enough, though. And at night, it could be pretty dark in there.

A narrow trail wound through the woods between their houses. Scott usually had a flashlight to help him find his way down the trail, but this time he had forgotten it.

So what, he thought. *I've been down that trail a zillion times.*

"See ya tomorrow at school," Scott said as he walked out the back door of Bridgette's house.

"Yeah. That is, *if* you make it home tonight," Bridgette teased.

The field in back of the house glowed with the bluish light of a full moon. The tall grass swayed softly as Scott walked toward the trail entrance at the edge of the woods. But as he got closer, the moon slipped behind a heavy cloud. Suddenly everything was pitch black, and where the trail disappeared into the woods, it was even blacker.

No big deal, Scott told himself. *Nothing's in those woods but squirrels and raccoons.*

At least he *hoped* that was all.

As he walked down the trail, Scott took his mind off the unwelcoming shadows by thinking about his checkers game. Bridgette was good, no doubt about it. But he didn't think it was hopeless that he might win the next game. *I'll challenge her to another game tomorrow,* he thought to himself.

Scott was nearly running through the forest that had never seemed so dangerous. He started thinking about how he had scared his little brother that morning. He replayed the events in his head.

"You'd better not go into my room," he had said to Logan. "A troll lives in there."

"Scott, you'd better stop scaring Logan," Bridgette scolded. "You got in big trouble the last time your mom caught you."

"But it's the only way to keep him out of my room!" Scott answered.

Scott loved his little brother. He was a cute little redhead with pudgy cheeks and a big, trusting smile. But the older he got, the more he got into Scott's things. And a guy can have a lot of things by the time he's nine years old.

Scott saw a glow of light among the trees in front of him and suddenly stopped. He heard the sound of footsteps in dry leaves. They crunched closer and closer from the trail ahead of him. Then the sweep of a flashlight beam shone across his face.

Scott felt more scared than he had ever been in his life. His heart pounded, and he shook with fear.

A voice came from farther along the trail. "Scott? Scott, is that you?"

Heaving a sigh of relief, Scott called, "Mom. It's me! It's me!"

He ran toward her, knowing that she'd be pretty upset. But strangely, she just hugged him and told him that she had been very worried.

As they walked home together, Scott said, "You know what, Mom? From now on, Logan can play in my room any time he wants."

1.　**Read the following sentence from the passage.**

　　"Bridgette had been successful every time."

　　What does *successful* mean?

　　A.　having success

　　B.　without success

　　C.　worthy of success

　　D.　made from success

2.   **What is the root of the word *bluish*?**

_____

3.   **Read the following sentence from the passage.**

   "Suddenly everything was pitch black, and where the trail disappeared into the woods, it was even blacker."

   Which word has the same root word as *disappeared*?

   A.   distant

   B.   appealing

   C.   appearance

   D.   apply

4.   **Read the following sentence from the passage.**

   "As he walked down the trail, Scott took his mind off the unwelcoming shadows by thinking about his checkers game."

   What does *unwelcoming* mean?

   _____

   _____

5. **Read the following sentence from the passage.**

    "I'll challenge her to another game tomorrow, he thought to himself."

    What does *challenge* most likely mean?

    _____

6. **Read the following sentence from the passage.**

    "Scott was nearly running through the forest that had never seemed so dangerous."

    What does *dangerous* mean?

    A. putting in danger
    B. lack of danger
    C. full of danger
    D. like danger

7. **Read the following sentence from the passage.**

    "He replayed the events in his head."

    What does *replayed* most likely mean?

    _____

    _____

8. **In the passage, Scott heaves "a sigh of relief." Which of the following words makes the same *ie* sound as *relief*?**

    A. lie
    B. tried
    C. spies
    D. thieves

Lesson 2: Word Meaning

Whether you're reading for school or for fun, it is likely that you will *encounter* (come across) an *unfamiliar* (strange or unknown) word or *phrase* (group of words) once in a while. Don't get *befuddled* (confused). With a few simple *strategies* (plans of attack), you can *decipher* (figure out the meaning of) almost any word or phrase you run into.

TIP 1: Look at the words around the unknown word.

Some multiple-choice questions will ask you about the meaning of a word. If you don't know what the word means, go back to the reading passage and find the word or phrase. Reread the whole sentence. You may even need to read the whole paragraph. The words around the unknown word will give you hints to the word's meaning. These hints are called **context clues**.

You can use these clues to make sure you understood a word correctly. Often when we first read an unfamiliar word, we think it's actually a different word that we already know. If you're reading quickly, you might not notice your mistake. But if the words around the unknown word don't make sense together, go back and reread. Check that you recognized the word, and figure out if it means what you thought it meant.

TIP 2: You can find the meaning of an unknown word in a series by looking at the other words in that series.

Words in a list often give you clues to the meaning of a new word. Read the following paragraph, then answer Numbers 1 and 2.

> Throughout the state, there are growths of lilies, daisies, violets, and <u>asters</u>. It is also home to jays, swallows, robins, <u>grackles</u>, and crows.

1. What is an aster?

   A. an animal

   B. a lake

   C. a flower

   D. a fish

2. What are grackles?

   A. cats

   B. dogs

   C. bugs

   D. birds

CCSs: RF.4.4c, L.4.4a, L.4.5c

 TIP 3: Look for when an author explains a word or repeats an idea in another way.

Some context clues are not as easy to see as others. Read the short passage that follows, then answer Numbers 3 and 4.

> Carmen nervously held the letter in her hand. It was from the *Poet's Corner*. She had entered her poem into their contest weeks ago. She wanted to win more than anything. Her heart was beating fast with excitement as she opened the envelope. Carmen unfolded the letter and read the first sentence: *We are pleased to announce that your poem is the first-place winner*. Carmen was <u>ecstatic</u>! She twirled around and clapped her hands with joy.

3. Think about how Carmen feels after winning the poetry contest. Now read the following sentences from the passage.

    "Carmen was <u>ecstatic</u>! She twirled around and clapped her hands with joy."

    What does the word *ecstatic* mean?

    A. very loud
    B. very happy
    C. very upset
    D. very confused

4. Which words from the passage helped you to know the answer to Number 3?

_____

 TIP 4: Look for other words with like meanings.

If you read carefully, you might find other words in the passage that have about the same meaning as the unknown word or phrase. **Synonyms** are words that mean about the same thing.

Read the following passage from *The Summer of the Swans* by Betsy Byars. It tells about a girl named Sara who enjoys watching movies on television.

> She was good, too, at joining in the <u>dialogue</u> with the actors. When the cowboy would say something like, "Things are quiet around here tonight," she would join in with, "Yeah, *too* quiet," right on cue.

5. Think about what Sara does. Then read this sentence from the passage.

   "She was good, too, at joining in the <u>dialogue</u> with the actors."

   What does the word *dialogue* mean?

   A. picture

   B. talk

   C. action

   D. fun

The passage tells that a cowboy would "say something" and that Sara "would join in." To *say something* and to *join in* by speaking are both talking. You can probably guess that *dialogue* means "spoken words" or "talk."

TIP 5: Look for words with opposite meanings.

Sometimes the passage will give you clues to the opposite meaning of an unknown word. An **antonym** is a word that means the opposite of another word.

Read the following paragraph. Then answer Numbers 6 and 7.

   The climate of most southern states is very <u>humid</u>. This is different from the climate of the southwestern states, which is very dry.

6. Underline a word in the paragraph that means the opposite of *humid*.

7. Now, reread this sentence from the paragraph.

   The climate of most southern states is very <u>humid</u>.

   What does the word *humid* mean?

   A. cold

   B. damp

   C. dusty

   D. snowy

CCSs: RF.4.4c, L.4.4a, L.4.4c

 TIP 6: Plug in the answer choices.

Many questions about vocabulary give you four answer choices. Try plugging each choice into the sentence in place of the unknown word or phrase. The one that makes the most sense in the passage should be the correct answer. This is also a great way to check your work.

Read the following passage.

> Rosita's heart <u>ached</u> with sorrow. Her best friend, Monty, was leaving town. His new home was a ranch out West. Would she ever get over the pain of his leaving?

Read Number 8, but don't answer it yet.

8. Read this sentence from the passage.

   Rosita's heart <u>ached</u> with sorrow.

   What does the word *ached* mean?

   A. hurt

   B. pounded

   C. beat

   D. thumped

First, plug each answer choice into the sentence in place of the word *ached*.

   A. Rosita's heart <u>hurt</u> with sorrow.

   B. Rosita's heart <u>pounded</u> with sorrow.

   C. Rosita's heart <u>beat</u> with sorrow.

   D. Rosita's heart <u>thumped</u> with sorrow.

Now go back and answer Number 8.

9. Which words from the passage helped you know the correct answer?

_____

 TIP 7: Use a dictionary to find out what a word means, how to spell it, and how to say it.

A **dictionary** is a list of word meanings. It may be a book, a Web site, or a computer program. A dictionary explains how to pronounce each word and what the word means. It may show the word used in a sentence. It lists words in alphabetical order so you can easily find them. (You can find a word on a dictionary Web site or computer program by typing it in a search box.)

Use the dictionary page to answer Numbers 10 and 11.

coo • core   129

a hat	**i** it	**oi** oil	**ch** child	**a** in about
ā age	**ī** ice	**ou** out	**ng** long	**e** in taken
ä far	**o** hot	**u** cup	**sh** she	**i** in pencil
e let	**ō** open	**u̇** put	**th** thin	**o** in lemon
ē equal	**ô** order	**ü** rule	**ᴛʜ** then	**u** in circus
ėr term			**zh** measure	

ə = (bracket grouping the right column)

coo (kü), ¹*noun* the sound made by a pigeon or dove. ²*verb* to make this sound.

cook (ku̇k), ¹*verb* to prepare food using heat. ²*verb* to go through the cooking process; to be cooked. ³*noun* a person who cooks food.

cook•ie (ku̇k′ē), *noun* a sweet, round, usually hard, flat cake.

cool (kül), ¹*adjective* more cold than warm. ²*adjective* giving a feeling of coolness: *a cool breeze*. ³*adjective* calm, not worried or excited: *a cool head*. ⁴*verb* to make cool: *cool with ice*.

coop (küp), ¹*noun* a small cage for animals: *a chicken coop*. ²*verb* to keep in a coop.

co•op•e•rate (kō-′ä-pə-,rāt), *verb* to work together as a team.

co•pi•lot (kō′pī lət), *noun* the second pilot on an airplane.

cop•per (kop′ər), ¹*noun* a reddish brown metal. ²*adjective* made of copper. ³*noun* a coin made from copper; a penny.

10. How many definitions does this dictionary give for the word *cool*?

    A. 1

    B. 2

    C. 3

    D. 4

11. In which of the following ways can the word *cook* be used?

    A. as a noun and a verb

    B. as a verb and an adjective

    C. as a noun and an adjective

    D. as an adjective and an adverb

TIP 8: Use a thesaurus to find synonyms and antonyms for words.

The word *thesaurus* sounds like a type of dinosaur. But a **thesaurus** is actually a tool for finding synonyms and antonyms. (Remember, synonyms are words with meanings that are alike. Antonyms are words with opposite meanings.) Like a dictionary, a thesaurus can be a book, a Web site, or a computer program.

A thesaurus is like a dictionary because words are listed in alphabetical order. Here's how part of a thesaurus page might look.

---

gift   (*n.*) present, favor, tip. See **GIVING.** *Ant.,* see **RECEIVING.**

glad   (*adj.*) happy, content, joyful, pleased. See **PLEASURE.** *Ant.,* see **SAD.**

go   (*v.*) leave, depart, withdraw, retire, exit; vanish, disappear; work, run. See **DEPARTURE, PASSAGE.** *Ant.,* see **ARRIVE.**

goof   (*n.*) error, mistake, slip-up. (*v.*) blunder, err.

To see how a thesaurus presents information, look under *gift* in the example. It suggests that you can find other words that are like *gift* by looking up *giving.* To find antonyms for *gift*, look up *receiving.*

Notice that the word *go* shows three different groups of words. The groups are separated by semicolons (;). Each group is made up of synonyms for a different meaning of *go.* Look at this sentence: "We will go at noon." Here, *go* means about the same as *leave, depart, withdraw, retire,* or *exit.* In the sentence "These machines go like this," *go* means the same as *work* or *run.*

When you choose a word from a thesaurus, be sure to read the words carefully. Not every synonym will make sense in every sentence. Be sure you pick the one that says what you are trying to say.

12. According to the thesaurus, what kind of word is *glad*?

A. noun

B. verb

C. adjective

D. both a noun and a verb

13. To find words that mean the opposite of *glad*, what word should you look up in the thesaurus?

    A. sad

    B. favor

    C. power

    D. pleasure

 TIP 9: Use the glossary.

Some books, such as social studies and science books, include a glossary. A **glossary** defines important words from the book. Like a dictionary, it is arranged in alphabetical order. It may list page numbers where those words appear. It is usually located in the back of the book.

When you are reading your social studies or science book, how do you know which words are in the glossary? Some books use boldface (**like this**) to highlight subject-area words in the text. In these books, bold words appear in the glossary. Other books may use italics (*like this*) for words in the text that appear in the glossary. You can use the glossary to learn the meaning of boldfaced and italicized words as you read.

When reading a passage, always pay attention to boldfaced or italicized words. If you can't figure out what the word means, check the glossary.

The following example is from the glossary of a book about spiders.

Glossary

A

abdomen—one of an arachnid's two main body parts (pages 4, 7)

arachnid—a small insect-like animal with two main body parts and eight legs (page 2)

B

bird spider—a very large South American spider that lives in trees and eats small birds (pages 6, 39, 51)

black widow—a small, poisonous spider with a shiny black body (pages 12, 43)

C

cephalothorax—one of the main parts of an arachnid's body, consisting of the head joined to the chest (pages 4, 11)

chelicerae—fang-like mouthparts that a spider uses to capture and kill its prey (pages 5, 25, 47)

CCSs: RI.4.4, L.4.4c, L.4.6

14. If you wanted to learn more about the black widow spider, which of these pages should you turn to?

  A. 6

  B. 39

  C. 43

  D. 51

TIP 10: Some school subjects use special words.

Some subjects use special words. You need to know those words to talk about the subject. For example, in science you might find words such as *wildlife*, *conservation*, or *endangered*. In math you might find words such as *radius*, *diameter*, or *multiplication*. In social studies you might see words such as *historical*, *society*, or *courts*.

When you read, try to figure out what these special words are and what they mean. Understanding these words can help you understand the subject.

Practice Activity

Directions: Look at the subject areas labeled A, B, and C below. Then write the letter for the correct subject on the line in front of each word that follows.

A—science **B—math** **C—social studies**

_____ climate	_____ governor	
_____ moon	_____ planets	
_____ equation	_____ senate	
_____ algebra	_____ estimation	
_____ Civil War	_____ bacteria	
_____ rounding	_____ Supreme Court	

TIP 11: Some words tell exact actions and emotions.

Part of growing as a reader is learning words that are more exact. For instance, you began by learning simple words like *hot* and *cold*. You later learned words like *fiery*, *icy*, *spicy*, and *chilly*. These words mean about the same as *hot* and *cold*, but they are more exact. How hot is the cocoa? *Piping*. How cold is the wind? *Brisk*. These words tell you more than *hot* and *cold*.

Exact words can show actions and feelings, too. For Numbers 15 through 17, write what the underlined word means.

15. After Lana got home, her friends <u>quizzed</u> her for hours about Paris.

_____

16. Jeremy <u>whined</u> all weekend about missing Friday's big game.

_____

17. When I met my first movie star, I just <u>stammered</u> a few words about being a fan.

_____

 TIP 12: Watch out for words that mean almost the same thing but show different feelings.

Synonyms mean *almost* the same thing, but they can be different in big ways. The differences are called shades of meaning. **Shades of meaning** are different feelings that go with the same basic meaning. For example, the words *loud* and *blaring* mean almost the same thing. But the word *blaring* has a bad feeling.

Look at these two examples:

The crowd gave a <u>loud</u> cheer when the band took the stage.

But the <u>blaring</u> music hurt Maxine's ears, so she left the concert.

As you can see, *blaring* does not just mean "loud." It means "too loud."

18. Which word or phrase means the same as *smart* but has a bad feeling?

    A. bright
    B. know-it-all
    C. knowledgeable
    D. clever

19. Which word means the same as *curious* but has a bad feeling?

    A. questioning
    B. nosy
    C. interested
    D. eager

Lesson Practice begins on the following page.

Directions: This passage is about a girl whose unusual pet causes trouble at the dinner table. Read the passage. Then answer Numbers 1 through 8.

Dilly Comes to Dinner

"Good grief, Samarra! What's that?" Dad asked. On the table next to Samarra's plate was a very large, very plump frog.

"Ribbitt," the frog croaked.

Samarra giggled at the look on her father's face. She said, "It's just my frog, Dad. His name's Dilly because his skin is green like a pickle. I found him in the park today. He looked starved, so I decided to give him something to eat."

"Hold your horses, young lady. No frog is going to be at our table during dinner," her father said.

"Your dad's right," her mom said as she dished up the mashed potatoes. "I think you'd better put Dilly somewhere a little safer. Somebody might get a taste for a pickle and take a bite out of him." She laughed at her own joke.

Samarra and Dad let out a groan at the same time. Mom was always trying to make jokes, but they usually weren't funny.

Samarra knew she'd better pick up her new pet. But Dilly knew she was after him, and he was too fast for her. He jumped over her right arm and landed in the salad.

"YUCK!" her father said.

"Oh, for goodness sake!" her mother said. "This frog is a pain in the neck!"

"Dilly!" Samarra cried. She leaned over the table and grabbed the salad bowl. "I've captured you now!"

But once again Dilly was too quick. He hopped out of the salad and into the mashed potatoes. They must have been too hot, because he didn't stay there long. Next, Dilly sprang onto the fried chicken. It was too hot as well. With a powerful leap, he landed in the lemonade pitcher.

Dad rose from his chair, quickly picked up the pitcher, and carried it to the sink. He poured out the lemonade and carefully held the slippery frog under the faucet to rinse him off.

Mom and Samarra looked at the salad. They looked at the mashed potatoes. They looked at Dad as he walked to the kitchen door and put the freshly washed Dilly outside. Then everybody looked at each other.

"I suddenly have a desire for pizza," Mom said.

This time everybody laughed.

1. In the passage, Samarra says, "He looked starved, so I decided to give him something to eat." What does *starved* mean?

   A. dangerous

   B. small

   C. hungry

   D. friendly

2. Read the following sentence from the passage.

   "Samarra giggled at the look on her father's face."

   What does *giggled* mean?

   A. worried

   B. frowned

   C. laughed

   D. thought

3. In the passage, the author writes, "Samarra and Dad let out a groan at the same time." What does *groan* mean?

   _____

   _____

4. Based on the passage, what does the word *captured* <u>most likely</u> mean?

   A. fed

   B. chased

   C. freed

   D. caught

5. **Read this sentence from the passage.**

   "On the table next to Samarra's plate was a very large, very plump frog."

   What does the word *plump* mean?

   _____

   _____

6. **Based on the passage, what does the word *sprang* <u>most likely</u> mean?**

   A. walked

   B. jumped

   C. danced

   D. called

7. **What is the root of the word *powerful*?**

   _____

8. **Read this sentence from the passage.**

   "'I suddenly have a desire for pizza,' Mom said."

   What does the word *desire* mean?

   A. need

   B. recipe

   C. dislike

   D. feeling

Lesson 3: Main Idea and Details

Imagine your friend asks you what you are reading. You say, "It's a really creepy story about . . ." You might not know it, but you are telling the main idea.

The **main idea** of a reading passage is what the passage is mostly about. Sometimes the author puts the main idea in a sentence. Sometimes you have to figure it out on your own.

Details are the facts and descriptions that make a reading passage more interesting. Without details, reading would be very boring.

Read the following paragraph from *About Animals*, published by World Book-Childcraft International.

> You can always tell a turtle by its shell. A box turtle has a high, round shell that it can close up like a box. A map turtle has a wide, flat shell with bumpy edges. A soft-shelled turtle's shell looks like a green pancake.

1. Find the sentence that tells what the paragraph is mostly about. Underline it.

Sometimes the main idea isn't given to you in one sentence. You might have to read the passage and figure out the main idea on your own.

Read the following paragraph from *A Cricket in Times Square* by George Selden. Then write a sentence that tells the main idea.

> "Catch the mouse!" shouted Mama. She picked up a *Fortune* magazine— very big and heavy—and heaved it after Tucker. It hit him on the left hind leg just as he vanished into the drain pipe.

2. What is the main idea of the paragraph?

_____

_____

_____

CCSs: RI.4.2, RI.4.10

➤ TIP 1: Read the whole passage first.

Before you can be sure about the main idea, you must read the whole passage first. Sometimes an idea might seem important, but when you get to the next paragraph, you find the author has moved on to a new thought. When you finish reading the whole passage, then you'll be able to see what the main idea is. Each paragraph should have something to say about the main idea. That's why you need to read the whole passage to figure out the main idea.

➤ TIP 2: Look for the main idea at the beginning or end of a passage.

If the passage has only one paragraph, the main idea can sometimes be found in the first or last sentence. If the passage has more than one paragraph, the main idea might introduce the topic in the first paragraph. Or, it might sum up the topic in the concluding, or final, paragraph. The main idea won't always be at the beginning or end of a passage, but these are good places to look for it.

➤ TIP 3: Find the details that support or explain the main idea.

The most important details support the main idea or help to explain it. To understand which details are important, you first need to know the main idea of the passage. Let's start by looking at the following short passage about kazoos.

The Story of the Kazoo
by John Ham

One of the easiest instruments to play is the kazoo. Simply place the wide end to your lips and hum. The humming causes a thin piece of film to shake. This shaking makes the buzzing sound of the kazoo.

The kazoo is based on an old African instrument. People used kazoos to mask their voices. When Africans came to America, they made these instruments. They used them to play music.

In the 1840s, an African American created the kazoo. His name was Alabama Vest. Vest drew the plans for the kazoo. Then a clockmaker made it from metal. The men showed it off at a state fair in 1852, and soon after, the instrument became widely used in the South.

Emil Sorg, a traveling salesman, met Vest on one of his trips. He became interested in selling the kazoo. With a partner, Sorg opened a kazoo factory in 1914. It was called the American Kazoo Company. It sold kazoos around the country. It still makes kazoos today.

3. What is the main idea of the passage?

_____

_____

_____

_____

The main idea of a reading passage is like the roof of a house. The main idea is supported by details in the passage, just as a roof is supported by walls. Walls that don't reach the ceiling can't support the roof. In the same way, details that have nothing to do with the main idea can't support the main idea. If the details don't support the main idea, then those details aren't important.

4. In the graphic organizer, write two other important details that support the main idea of the passage.

MAIN IDEA

Alabama Vest based the kazoo on an African instrument

Supporting Detail	Supporting Detail	Supporting Detail
• An African instrument used to mask the voice.		

38

CCSs: RL.4.1, RL.4.10

Read the following story. It will help you understand the tips that follow.

Gramps and Me

by Peter S. Douglas

When I was ten, my grandfather came to live with my family. I'd never even seen him before. He was a stranger to me. Mom said that for 25 years he'd been the foreman on a cattle ranch in California. When Gramps showed up, I was surprised. He seemed too young to be 80. He walked easily without a cane, though he did have a walking stick.

Just about all Gramps did that first week was whittle his walking stick. He sat on the back porch wearing a cowboy hat that looked too big for him. He took a knife out of his pocket and began to carve at the stick's handle. He silently whittled away the hours while a pile of curled wood chips grew beside him.

One day after I got home from school, I found him rubbing his walking stick with a piece of fine sandpaper. "How's it going, Gramps?" I asked.

"Not so bad, Toby," he said. His big hat hid his face, but I could see his fingers working. When he blew the sawdust away, I saw the head of a horse carved into his stick.

"Wow!" I said.

"This is Paloma, the horse your grandmother and I had when we panned for gold."

"You really panned for gold?" I asked. Gramps was starting to look different to me. His hat didn't seem so big anymore. I sat down next to him as he worked.

"It was long before your time, Toby. Before your mother's, too," Gramps said. "Your Grandma Clara and I lived in an old canvas tent on the banks of a stream in the mountains. And no," he said, answering the unspoken question in my eyes, "we never did strike it rich. But Clara and I didn't mind. We made enough to get us to our next adventure."

"I suppose you went hunting for lost gold mines," I said, joking.

"Now, that's a whole other story," he said.

TIP 4: List the important parts of the passage.

If you can figure out what is important in the passage, you'll be able to state the main idea. On the following lines, write three important details of the story you just read.

5. _____

_____

6. _____

_____

7. _____

   _____

8. Think about the important details of the story you just listed. Use them to write the story's main idea on the following lines.

   _____

   _____

   _____

TIP 5: Summarize the events in the passage so the main idea is easier to find.

When you **summarize** the events in the passage, you tell its most basic ideas. You describe the events in sequence. **Sequence** is the order in which things happen. Retelling allows you to see the most important parts of the passage more easily, including the main idea and the details that support that idea.

9. Look back to the story "Gramps and Me." Which of the following provides the best summary?

   A. Gramps comes to live with Toby and his family when the boy is ten and Gramps is 80. Most of the time, Gramps sits around wearing a cowboy hat and whittling a stick.

   B. Gramps is 80 years old when he moves in with ten-year-old Toby and the boy's family. After Gramps starts telling Toby stories about his life, they begin to enjoy each other's company.

   C. Toby's grandfather once lived in the mountains. He and his wife, Clara, lived in a tent and panned for gold. They never got rich, but they made enough money to get to their next adventure.

   D. Toby's grandfather once had a horse named Paloma. During the first week that Gramps stays with Toby and the boy's family, Gramps carves the figure of Paloma's head onto a stick.

10. Describe two ways that Toby gets to know his grandfather. Use information from the story in your answer.

_____

_____

_____

_____

 TIP 6: Put together clues from the passage to make inferences.

Hidden messages are like mysteries. If you have only one clue, they're hard to figure out. The more clues you have, the easier it is to solve the mystery. In a reading passage, the details are the clues. In a made-up story, these details include what the characters say and do. In an article about true events, the clues are facts about real people and real events. When you **make an inference**, you gather all the clues from the passage and combine them with what you already know to figure out that hidden meaning.

Answer Numbers 11 and 12 to make an inference about how Toby feels when his grandfather first comes to stay.

11. Go back to the story and underline any clues that tell what Toby thinks about Gramps when he first arrives.

12. What does Toby think about Gramps when he first arrives?

    A. He is a close friend who tells interesting stories.

    B. He looks young and wastes his time whittling.

    C. He is talented at carving but a little scary.

    D. He does not belong here with Toby's family.

TIP 7: Draw conclusions based on what you have read.

After you have made inferences, you can come to a final decision about what you have read. The decision you make is called a **conclusion**. When you draw a conclusion, think carefully about the inferences you made and other details you have gathered from the passage. Then decide what else must be true. Something in the passage must help to explain your decision. By putting together your inferences and important details from the passage, you can draw a reasonable conclusion about what you've read.

13. How does Toby feel about Gramps at the beginning of the story? How do you know?

_____

_____

TIP 8: The theme of the passage connects the story to the reader.

Once you know the main idea, it becomes easier to determine the theme. The **theme** is an idea that is important for all people, not just those in the passage. You can think of the theme as the lesson the author wants readers to learn. The author doesn't usually say exactly what the theme is. You have to figure it out on your own.

For example, you probably know Aesop's fable about the race between the tortoise (turtle) and the hare (rabbit). The theme of that fable is this lesson: "We can succeed against great odds if we try very hard."

14. What important lesson does Toby learn in the story?

    A. Living a life of excitement and adventure can be difficult.

    B. Whittling is an easy hobby that anyone can do.

    C. Taking time to get to know someone can be rewarding.

    D. Mining for gold is hard work.

Lesson Practice begins on the following page.

Directions: This passage is about how footballs are made. Read the passage. Then answer Numbers 1 through 8.

Kick Me! I'm a Football

by Rick Zollo

Some people call me a pigskin, but I'm not made out of a pig. My cousins, the baseball, the basketball, and the soccer ball, are made in other countries. I'm made here in the United States, in the small town of Ada, Ohio. What am I?

Okay, so you read the title. I'm a football. But do you know how I'm made?

I'm made from cowhide rather than pigskin, and I'm cut from a pattern. The cowhide is just the outer layer. I have an inner lining made of plastic. At one time, our insides were made from pigs. That's how people came up with the name *pigskin*. Once my inside and outside are formed, the two linings are stitched together and filled with air. That's when I really start to look like a football.

All the footballs used in the National Football League (NFL) are made in Ada. To make it to the NFL, we have to be perfect. If we're a little less than perfect, we get sold to you, the regular customer. We've got to be the best to play with the big boys. It's a big responsibility being an NFL football.

To be considered perfect, we're put through a series of demanding tests, one after another. A worker fills us with air several times to make sure we don't leak. Another worker checks our seams to see that they're straight. If we're going to the NFL, we're required to be double-laced for strength. After all, if some 300-pound guy is going to jump on you, two laces are better than one. If we go to sporting goods stores, we get laced only once.

When we're sold—either to the NFL or to you, the regular customer—we're ready to be passed, handed off, and yes, kicked. I want to make it to the NFL, but I'll be just as grateful if I go to one of you. I might even have more fun playing in somebody's backyard than in some stadium. Wherever I go, I'm proud to be a football. So go ahead, kick me!

1. **What is this passage mostly about?**

    A. All NFL footballs are made in the same town.

    B. Perfectly made footballs go to the NFL, and the rest go to stores.

    C. Footballs are called pigskins even though they are made from cowhide.

    D. Most footballs made for the NFL go to sporting goods stores.

2. **What tests are used to decide whether a football is perfect? Write your answer in the form of a summary.**

    _____

    _____

    _____

3. **Which sentence from the passage supports the idea that few footballs make it to the NFL?**

    A. "Once my inside and outside are formed, the two linings are stitched together and filled with air."

    B. "We've got to be the best to play with the big boys."

    C. "A worker fills us with air several times to make sure we don't leak."

    D. "I might even have more fun playing in somebody's backyard than in some stadium."

4. **What kinds of layers are used to make a football?**

    _____

    _____

5.   **Read the following sentence from the passage.**

"I'm made from cowhide rather than pigskin, and I'm cut from a pattern."

Which of the following meanings of *pattern* is used in the sentence?

A.   a cloth with a repeating picture printed on it

B.   a set of matching dishes and silverware

C.   the flight path used to land an airplane

D.   a guide used to make each item the same

6.   **What is one way a football can be less than perfect?**

_____

_____

_____

7.   **What is the last step in making a football?**

A.   A pattern is cut from cowhide.

B.   An inner lining is made out of plastic.

C.   The two linings are filled with air.

D.   The inner and outer linings are sewed together.

8.   **According to the passage, footballs are "put through a series of demanding tests." What does the word *series* mean?**

_____

_____

CCS: RF.4.4a

Lesson 4: Getting the Most from What You Read

"Martha, I've read this story a dozen times or more, and I'm still not sure what's going on. I think I'll wait until someone makes it into a movie!"

Do you ever have trouble understanding what you read? Everybody has this problem at some time or another. Good readers know a few tips that help them get the most from what they're reading. After you finish this lesson, you'll know those tips, too.

TIP 1: Ask yourself, "Why am I reading this?"

Your reason for reading can affect the way you read. Before reading, ask yourself, "Why am I reading this?" Are you doing your homework, or are you reading *TV Guide* to see what comes on at 7:00 P.M.? Are you reading for enjoyment or just to pass the time? You need to adjust the way you look at a selection of text based on your reason for reading. If you are reading for fun, you might read more quickly. Reading for a school assignment or a test is a different matter.

When you read a school assignment, you will be reading to find out information. Don't rush on your first read, but don't go too slowly either. You want to understand the overall picture, and taking too much time to read might make you more confused, as details and main ideas begin to blur together. Instead, when you are finished, skim the passage again to remind yourself of important points by looking for them specially. To **skim** means to run your eyes over the passage to look for important ideas. The following tips discuss other good ways to get the most out of your reading.

TIP 2: Preview the passage.

You can "warm up" for reading by previewing the passage before jumping right in. **Previewing** means looking over a passage before you really read it. Previewing will give you an idea of what to expect and can help you understand the passage better. You will probably remember more of it later, too.

Here's how to preview:

- Look at the **title**.

- Look at the **table of contents** and **index** in nonfiction books.

- Look at the **headings** and **subheadings**. Headings and subheadings are the words or phrases that tell you what parts of a passage are about. In a book, look for chapter headings that break the book into parts. You will learn more about headings and subheadings in Tip 3.

- Read any words in *italics,* **bold print**, CAPITAL LETTERS, or <u>underlined</u> print. These special types of print tell you that the words are important. They may tell you something about the main idea. Remember, the **main idea** of a passage is what it is mostly about.

- Look at any **illustrations**, **diagrams**, **photos**, or **tables**. Also read the words beneath or beside the illustrations. Ask yourself, "Why did the author include these? How do they tell me more about the topic?"

- When previewing a passage, read the first sentence of each paragraph. The first sentence usually tells what the whole paragraph is about. You can spot paragraphs by looking for indents. An **indent** is a gap at the start of a sentence. It shows that a new paragraph has started.

Take a few minutes to preview "Tarantula!" on page 49 before moving on to the next tip.

TIP 3: Use headings to find key ideas in a passage.

Headings, or subheadings, are usually in smaller type than passage titles. Headings help show you where different ideas are located in the passage. They can help you find certain information more quickly. Headings and subheadings are often used to mean the same thing, but headings generally let the reader know about a bigger topic. When a topic needs to be broken into smaller ideas, subheadings are used. For instance, in this lesson, the heading "Lesson 4: Getting the Most from What You Read" tells you what the main topic is. The "Tips," or subheadings, give you more information about that topic. You can use both headings and subheadings to quickly find information in a passage.

For example, let's say an author wrote a passage about the life of Abraham Lincoln and used the following subheadings.

School Days and Home Life

Abe Becomes Head of a Post Office

Teaching Himself About Laws

Lincoln Becomes Sixteenth President

The War Years

1. Under which subheading could the reader learn about Lincoln working with the U.S. mail?

   A. The War Years

   B. School Days and Home Life

   C. Abe Becomes Head of a Post Office

   D. Teaching Himself About Laws

TIP 4: Ask questions before you read.

Once you have previewed the passage, think about what you might find out once you start reading. Here are a few questions to guide you.

- What do you think the subject of the passage will be?

- How is the passage organized? Does the author tell about events in the order in which they happen? Or are two things compared, showing how they are alike and different?

- What type of writing is it? Is it a made-up story; a story about real people, places, and ideas; a play; or a poem?

- Why did the author write it? Does the author want to entertain you, inform or teach you, convince you, or simply share his or her ideas and experiences?

- What do you expect to learn from the passage? What kinds of questions do you think it will answer?

2. Preview the passage on pages 49 through 52. What do you predict it will be about?

_____

_____

CCSs: RI.4.10, RF.4.4a

Read the first two paragraphs of "Tarantula!" Then answer the question that follows.

Tarantula!

by Karen Nichols

Have you ever been frightened by a spider? Sometimes even little spiders look a bit creepy crawling around. But what about BIG, HAIRY spiders? Now those can be really scary!

Don't Judge a Book by Its Cover

The old saying "Don't judge a book by its cover" is true for spiders. Even some of the most scary-looking ones aren't nearly as harmful as you might think. One really scary-looking type of spider is the **tarantula**. It is one of those BIG, HAIRY spiders.

3. Now that you have read the first part of the passage, what do you think it is about?

_____

_____

Continue reading about tarantulas.

Big Spiders, Little Spiders

There are hundreds of different kinds of tarantulas in the world. The bird spider is a tarantula that lives in South America. This spider is very large. Its body, not counting its legs, can be as long as 3 1/2 inches. It is called a *bird spider* because it lives in trees and eats small birds. Some bird spiders in Brazil also eat small amphibians and reptiles.

The tarantula's bite helps it kill insects and other small animals for food. The bite of some kinds of tarantulas can make humans very sick. Most of these dangerous spiders (like the funnel-web spider of Australia) live in other parts of the world. Tarantulas that live in the United States are far less harmful to humans. To be bitten by one of these spiders wouldn't be much fun. But for the most part, it would be about as serious as being stung by a bee. That's right, although tarantulas are made to seem like very dangerous creatures in movies, people rarely die from tarantula bites.

The trap-door spider is found in the southwestern United States. It grows to be about an inch long. For its home, it digs a burrow in the ground. It covers this burrow with a hinged door made of mud and its own silk. It also lines the burrow with silk to make a comfortable nest for its young.

CCSs: RI.4.10, RF.4.4a

Parts of a Tarantula

pedipalps—used in mating

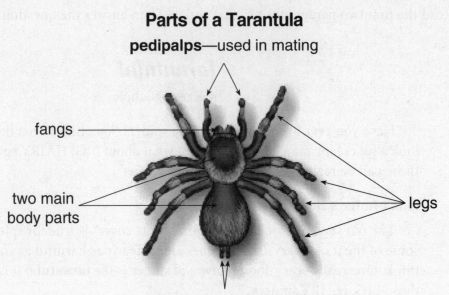

fangs

two main
body parts

legs

spinnerets—release silk

The trap-door spider is shy. Most females hardly ever leave their nests. They don't really have to. The trap-door spider simply waits just inside its burrow for a tasty animal to walk past. When it senses the footsteps of its victim, it throws open the door, grabs the animal, and poisons it. Then the tarantula drags its victim inside.

(To be continued . . .)

TIP 5: Ask questions as you read.

As you read, slow down to ask yourself, *Do I understand what the author is saying? Does this make sense? What will the writer say next?* You may also want to ask yourself other questions about the passage. What else would you like to know about the topic?

4. Based on what you have read so far, write one question about the passage. It can be about something you don't understand or something you would like to know more about.

_____

_____

CCSs: RI.4.1, RI.4.2, RF.4.4a

 TIP 6: Stop occasionally to retell or summarize.

When you are reading, stop now and then to summarize. When you summarize, you retell the main idea and most important points in your mind. If you have difficulty summarizing, then you may not fully understand the passage. You may want to go back and reread some parts of it.

5. Which of the following is the best summary of the section "Big Spiders, Little Spiders"?

    A. Bird spiders are very large. They live in South America and have bodies more than three inches long. They sometimes eat frogs.

    B. There are three main kinds of tarantulas. Some tarantulas are very small, and some are very large. Some are more dangerous than others. Tarantulas eat many things and are found on several continents.

    C. Tarantulas that live in the United States are much less dangerous to humans than the funnel-web spider that lives in Australia.

    D. The tarantula's bite helps it kill insects and small animals for food. The bite of some kinds of tarantulas can make humans very sick.

TIP 7: Use information from the text to draw inferences.

As you learned in Lesson 3, an **inference** is a guess you make based on clues from the passage. When an author doesn't come right out and say something, you may need to guess.

One thing you may need to figure out for yourself is why something happens. In "Tarantula!" the author says North American spiders' bites are not very dangerous to people. She does not explain exactly why that is true. But we can look for other details and use what we already know about bug bites to help us guess. She likens the bites to bee stings. From this we can guess that the bites contain only a little poison.

TIP 8: Study the graphics that go with the text.

Graphics are charts, graphs, drawings, photographs, and other artwork. Authors use them to explain their texts and make them clearer for the reader. Sometimes a picture can show something that is hard to say in words. Looking at graphics can help you understand a passage.

Look at the diagram of a tarantula on page 50, and then answer the question.

6. Where are the tarantula's pedipalps located?

    A. on its rear

    B. under its fangs

    C. on its head

    D. next to the spinnerets

Continue reading about tarantulas. Continue to ask questions and summarize as you read.

Eat or Be Eaten

> Tarantulas don't just eat. They are in danger of being eaten, too. Birds and mice try to kill them for food. Tarantulas even try to kill each other for food. But tarantulas have many ways to protect themselves. Sometimes they try to scare away their enemies. They stand up on their hind legs and rub their jaws together to make a loud hissing sound.

> Other tarantulas have an even stranger way to scare off animals looking for a furry meal. These tarantulas are covered with thousands of tiny hairs. The hairs fly off the tarantula's body and into the eyes, nose, and mouth of its attacker when the tarantula rubs its legs together. The hairs have tiny hooks on them, so you can imagine how pleasant this is for the tarantula's enemies!

Living for 20 Years or More

> Even with these great defenses, many young tarantulas are eaten by other animals. But tarantulas can live very long lives, some even 20 years or longer.

Lesson Practice begins on the following page.

Directions: This passage is about a famous bicyclist. Read the passage. Then answer Numbers 1 through 8.

Lance Armstrong Rides to Win

by Caroline Bruce

The Beginning

Lance Armstrong was a great athlete as a child. By the time he was 12, Armstrong was racing in triathlons against adults. (In a triathlon, the racers must swim, bike, and run.) Armstrong even won races against adults when he was still a kid.

Soon it was clear that biking was Armstrong's best sport. He began training only for bicycle races. His dream was to ride in the Tour de France. The Tour is the world's best-known bicycle race.

A Serious Setback

When Armstrong was 25, doctors told him he had cancer. That is a serious illness. The cancer was in many parts of Armstrong's body. The doctors said he had a 50-percent chance of living. He spent the next three years fighting the disease. Once he was healthy, doctors told Armstrong something surprising. He had actually had a 3-percent chance of living, not 50. They hadn't told him the truth at first because they didn't want him to lose hope.

The Biggest Race

The Tour de France is a three-week race that circles France. The race is made up of 22 stages. Each day is called a stage. The riders must go a certain distance in one day. This way, each day is a race that is part of the bigger race. At the end of each stage, the daily times are added up. The rider with the shortest time is called "the leader." The leader wears a yellow shirt the next day. At the end of the race, the rider with the shortest time wins.

Parts of the race go through the mountains of France. The mountains are hard to ride through. The race is a great test of strength and staying power.

Armstrong had done well on the Tour de France before he got cancer. He had won two stages: one in 1993 and one in 1995. In 1999, Armstrong returned to the race, ready to win it all. He had beaten the odds against cancer. Now Armstrong beat the other riders. He won the race by more than seven minutes.

Armstrong went on to win the Tour de France six more times in a row. In 2005, after his seventh win, Armstrong decided to stop racing for a living. But he returned in 2009 and this time took third place in the Tour de France. At 38, he was one of the oldest people ever to do so well.

Before Armstrong, four men had won the Tour de France five times. One had even won the race five times in a row. But no one else has come close to Armstrong's record of seven wins in a row.

Beyond the Records

If Lance Armstrong had never had cancer, he would still be famous. But Armstrong has used his fame to help other cancer patients. His yellow "Livestrong" wristbands are sold to raise money for research. He used his 2009 return to the Tour to bring attention to the disease.

No one knows what struggles might lay in store for Lance Armstrong. But he will surely meet them with the strength of a champion. Between his racing and his ability to beat cancer, Armstrong has already done amazing things!

1. **What is this passage <u>mostly</u> about?**

    A.   how the Tour de France is run

    B.   why doctors lied to Lance Armstrong

    C.   how Lance Armstrong became famous

    D.   what Lance Armstrong did to help others

2. **What information can be found in the section "The Biggest Race"?**

    A.   Lance Armstrong's early sports success

    B.   Armstrong's treatment for cancer

    C.   how Armstrong has helped cancer patients

    D.   the way riders win the Tour de France

3. What are the "Livestrong" bracelets used for?

    _____

    _____

4. Read these sentences from the passage.

    "Lance Armstrong was a great athlete as a child. By the time he was 12, Armstrong was racing in triathlons against adults."

    What does the word *athlete* <u>most likely</u> mean?

    _____

    _____

5. Why did doctors tell Armstrong he had a 50-percent chance of living through cancer?

    A. They didn't want him to lose hope.

    B. Their medical tests did not work properly.

    C. They didn't know they were wrong.

    D. Doctors are usually poor at math.

6. The passage says the Tour de France "is a great test of strength and staying power." What are two ways in which the race tests these things?

_____

_____

_____

_____

_____

7. Which word from the passage means about the same as *disease*?

A. cancer

B. illness

C. distance

D. patients

8. The author says Lance Armstrong would be famous even if he had never had cancer. Why would Armstrong still be famous?

_____

_____

CCS: RL.4.5

Lesson 5: Poetry, Prose, and Drama

The writing you have seen so far in this workbook is called prose. **Prose** is writing that has lines stretching from one end of the page to the other. Stories, novels, and articles are kinds of prose writing. There are two other types of writing: poetry and drama. In this lesson, you will learn about the differences between the three types of writing.

Poetry

Poetry is a special kind of writing. Unlike prose, the words send a message to the reader in a musical sort of way. Poems come in many forms. The following tips will tell you about the elements of poetry.

TIP 1: Poems are made up of lines and stanzas.

A **line** is a row of words. In prose, sometimes a sentence is a line. Other times a sentence is split into more than one line. Sentences in poems can be in one line or split across a few lines. Prose is broken into paragraphs. Each paragraph has a main idea and details that support it. Some poems are broken into stanzas. A **stanza** is a group of lines. The lines are often grouped together by how the lines rhyme. Often each stanza has the same number of lines. A blank line appears between stanzas.

TIP 2: Some poems have end words that rhyme.

Poems are different from prose because sometimes lines rhyme. Words that **rhyme** have the same end sound. Many poems use rhyming words at the end of the lines. Most rhyming words end with the same vowel sound and often with the same final consonant. Here are some examples of rhyming words:

feet / sheet   rap / cap   goat / coat

1. Write a word that rhymes with each of the following.

    cat _____ house _____

    tree _____ show _____

    pool _____ shoe _____

Usually, each stanza of a poem repeats the same rhyme pattern. Mother Goose poems are good examples of poems with end rhymes.

Read this part of a poem. Think about which words rhyme.

from

My Shadow

by Robert Louis Stevenson

I have a little shadow that goes in and out with me,
And what can be the use of him is more than I can see.
He is very, very like me from the heels up to the head;
And I see him jump before me, when I jump into bed.

The funniest thing about him is the way he likes to grow—
Not at all like proper children, which is always very slow;
For he sometimes shoots up taller like an India-rubber ball,
And he sometimes gets so little that there's none of him at all.

2. How many sentences are used in the first stanza?

   A. 1

   B. 2

   C. 3

   D. 4

3. What is the rhyme pattern of "My Shadow"?

   A. Every line rhymes.

   B. Every third line rhymes.

   C. Every other line rhymes.

   D. Every pair of lines rhyme.

4. Which word rhymes with *head*?

   A. me

   B. see

   C. bed

   D. can

CCSs: RL.4.5, RL.4.10

TIP 3: Many poems have a musical rhythm.

Think of your favorite pop music song. Does it make you want to dance to the beat? If so, the song has rhythm. In poetry, **rhythm** means that the sounds of words create a pattern.

How can words create a pattern? Some sounds in each word are stressed, or said more strongly. Each sound is called a syllable. For example, the word *wonder* has two syllables: won / der. The won syllable is stressed. It is said more loudly than the der.

To make rhythm, poets choose words based on which syllables are stressed. They may choose words that sound like this: TUM-ta. Here, the first syllable is stressed. Or they may use words that sound like this: ta-TUM. Here, the second syllable is stressed. A poet could use one of these patterns to make a line with rhythm:

> ta-TUM ta-TUM ta-TUM ta-TUM

Now, let's use some real words to show rhythm.

> The **moon**lit **night** was **warm** and **bright**.

Can you hear the pattern of stressed and soft syllables? Now read the poem below. The words of the poem are marked to show the stressed syllables. Those syllables are in **bold** type. Notice that each line has four stressed syllables.

Listen for the rhythm as you read this poem quietly to yourself.

The Woodpecker

by Elizabeth Madox Roberts

> The **wood**pecker **pecked** out a **lit**tle round **hole**
> And **made** him a **house** in the **tel**ephone **pole**.
> One **day** when I **watched** he **poked** out his **head**,
> And he **had** on a **hood** and a **col**lar of **red**.
> When **streams** of **rain** pour **out** of the **sky**,
> And the **spark**les of **light**ning go **flash**ing **by**,
> And the **big**, big **wheels** of **thun**der **roll**,
> He can **snug**gle **back** in the **tel**ephone **pole**.

Well-written prose has rhythm, too. What is different, though, is that the rhythm does not just come from the sound of the words. Authors of prose create rhythm by including different types of sentences in a paragraph. A mixture of shorter and longer sentences creates a rhythm. The rhythm that words and sentences make helps create emotion for the reader.

TIP 4: Poets often repeat words, phrases, lines, or whole stanzas.

To repeat is to do something over. Poetry often uses repeated words. Repeating helps create rhythm in some poems. It may also help show the important ideas and make a poem easier to remember. Look at these examples from nursery rhymes.

Pat-a-cake, pat-a-cake, baker's man.

Row, row, row your boat . . .

Hickory, dickory, dock,
The mouse ran up the clock;
The clock struck one,
The mouse ran down;
Hickory, dickory, dock.

Read the poem and answer the question that follows.

Tired Tim

by Walter de la Mare

Poor tired Tim! It's sad for him.
He lags the long bright morning through,
Ever so tired of nothing to do;
He moons and mopes the livelong day,
Nothing to think about, nothing to say;
Up to bed with his candle to creep,
Too tired to yawn, too tired to sleep:
Poor tired Tim! It's sad for him.

5. Which line is repeated in the poem?

A. He lags the long bright morning through,

B. Ever so tired of nothing to do;

C. He moons and mopes the livelong day,

D. Poor tired Tim! It's sad for him.

It's a poem! It's a story! It's—a narrative poem!

Narrative poems are a little more like stories than other poems are. They have beginnings, middles, and ends. For example, "The Woodpecker" tells a story, doesn't it? A woodpecker makes a house for himself and snuggles in his home when it rains. But "The Woodpecker" is still very much a poem, too. It has rhythm, and it is told using stanzas instead of paragraphs.

CCS: RL.4.5

TIP 5: Poets often use alliteration, assonance, and onomatopoeia.

Alliteration is the use of words that begin with the same consonant sound. Alliteration helps give writing a special musical sound. Here are some examples of alliteration at work:

> Peter Piper picked a peck of pickled peppers.

> She sells seashells by the seashore.

Prose writers sometimes use alliteration, but not as often as writers of poetry do. Here's an example of alliteration from the *Wizard of Oz*.

> "Which road leads to the Wicked Witch of the West?" asked Dorothy.
> "There is no road," answered the Guardian of the Gates. "No one ever wishes to go that way."

Assonance is the use of words that have the same vowel sound. Here are some examples:

> Joe hoped he could joke about his broken bone.

> In June, the duke bought two new flutes and a blue tuba.

Though prose might sometimes contain assonance, it is more often a feature of poetry.

Onomatopoeia is using words that sound like what they mean. Here are some examples:

> moo   hiss   buzz   meow   plop   sizzle

Poets often use many of these words together to help readers more fully imagine the sounds.

> The splash, the gush, the whisper of water
> and the whistling whoosh of hissing winds,
> splattering, battering the leaves and rooftops—
> the rumble and grumble as thunder begins.

Prose writers also use onomatopoeia, but not usually so heavily. Compare this example to the rainstorm example:

> Outside, Elena could hear the first whispers of rain drizzling on the distant trees. Soon the water began to splash in puddles and the wind began to rush. Finally, dull rumbles warned of the cloudburst to come.

Read the poem below, and answer the questions that follow.

Shade and Shadow

by Mike Acton

I heard a cricket creaking
As I stood in silence peeking
Down a long and narrow pathway to the village through the trees.
Then I saw a wee bug flashing
As its little wings went thrashing
And its greenish flame winked off and on a dozen times at me.

I heard an owl calling
(As the evening dew was falling)
From the black and brittle branches of an ancient, brooding tree.
The moon made shade and shadow
Through the oaks, and though I had no
Cause to stop, I paused to hear the night winds sighing over me.

And I noted, slowly poking
Down the lane, a chorus croaking
As a hundred frogs together sang along the silver stream.
Through the trees bright stars were winking,
And I paused in silence thinking
Life is full of greater beauty than the sweetest of our dreams.

6. Which of the following lines from the poem is the best example of alliteration?

   A.   Then I saw a wee bug flashing

   B.   And its greenish flame winked off and on a dozen times at me.

   C.   From the black and brittle branches of an ancient, brooding tree.

   D.   Life is full of greater beauty than the sweetest of our dreams.

7. Which of the following lines from the poem is the best example of assonance?

    A. I heard an owl calling

    B. (As the evening dew was falling)

    C. And I noted, slowly poking

    D. Through the trees bright stars were winking,

8. Which of the following lines from the poem has an example of onomatopoeia?

    A. I heard a cricket creaking

    B. The moon made shade and shadow

    C. Through the oaks, and though I had no

    D. And I paused in silence thinking

9. Write two more examples of alliteration from the poem.

    _____

    _____

 TIP 6: Some poems are written in free verse.

Free verse is poetry that does not have a set pattern of rhythm or rhyme. It depends on the natural rhythm of the language to make its music. This doesn't mean that free verse won't *ever* have end rhyme. Sometimes it will. Sometimes parts of a free-verse poem will have a set rhythm, too. But there will be no pattern of rhyme or rhythm through the whole poem.

Look at the poem on page 64. The poet doesn't make the lines rhyme. He doesn't use a set rhythm or lines of the same length. Still, the poem paints clear pictures in our minds. It makes its own special music. The poet has chosen the words and placed them on the page to create his own effect.

Read the poem and answer the questions that follow.

Theme in Yellow
by Carl Sandburg

I spot the hills
With yellow balls in autumn.
I light the prairie cornfields
Orange and tawny gold clusters
And I am called pumpkins.
On the last of October
When dusk is fallen
Children join hands
And circle round me
Singing ghost songs
And love to the harvest moon;
I am a jack-o'-lantern
With terrible teeth
And the children know
I am fooling.

10. Place a checkmark next to each line that has only four syllables.

11. Circle any end-rhyme words. If there are no end rhymes, write "None" on the line below.

_____

 TIP 7: A pattern of rhythm is called meter.

You have seen how a poet uses words to create rhythm. **Meter** is a pattern of rhythm that repeats throughout the poem. Each use of the pattern is called a **foot**. A foot may take many forms:

ta-TUM (one unstressed syllable, one stressed syllable)

TUM-ta (one stressed syllable, one unstressed syllable)

ta-ta-TUM (two unstressed syllables, one stressed syllable)

TUM-ta-ta (one stressed syllable, two unstressed syllables)

And so on. Often, a poem will include four or five feet in a line. Look at the following example.

> In a **house** in the **woods** on a **bright**, sunny **day**,
> seven **mice** made a **kite** and then **flew** it a**way**.

12. How many feet are used in each line?

   A. 1

   B. 2

   C. 3

   D. 4

Meter is not used in prose. Sentences and paragraphs, like free verse, may have their own rhythms. But no pattern controls the rhythm of an entire story.

TIP 8: Read prose and poems aloud with feeling.

When you are asked to read prose and poetry aloud, follow the rhythm of the words. Speak carefully so you do not trip over words. Speak slowly enough so that your words do not run together. But you should also speak with energy. Don't slow down to a crawl unless the story or poem calls for it. Last, understand the feeling of what you are reading. Put that feeling into your voice.

Drama

Drama is a kind of story that is meant to be performed by actors. It includes plays, movies, and TV shows. **Plays** are dramas acted out in front of a live audience. Drama is written in the form of a script. A **script** tells actors what to say and do, but it does not include many details because the audience will not read it.

Playwrights are writers of plays. Their job is not the same as the job of fiction writers. Most prose writers include lots of information about their characters. They tell what the characters look like, how they dress, and so on. They also have to explain the settings of their stories, such as the time of day and the place. A playwright doesn't have to tell about these things. The audience can see the characters and settings for themselves.

Drama is very different from poetry. Writers of poetry use words to create pictures in readers' minds. Drama uses spoken words, scenery, and objects to show audiences what happens in a story.

TIP 9: A play is divided into acts and scenes.

Plays are often broken into acts and scenes. A **scene** is made up of all the action that occurs in a given place and time. If the place or time changes, a new scene begins. The change of scenes is usually shown by the stage lights going dark. An **act** is a group of scenes. Plays may include one act or several.

Prose writers often use chapters to split up scenes or sections of a story. They do not label scenes, but blend one into the next. Poetry is much shorter than drama and prose, and its parts are often broken into stanzas.

 TIP 10: Plays do not explain as much as stories.

As you have learned, scripts do not include many details. The audience members can see the characters and the set for themselves. Also, prose writers can tell readers how characters feel and think. Playwrights cannot do this. Instead, all of these things must be shown by what the actors do and say.

Playwrights usually explain what the set should look like. The director uses this information to build the set. The information is often simple and leaves many choices up to the director.

13. Give two reasons that plays explain characters and settings less than stories do.

_____

_____

_____

> ### More Drama Terms
>
> **cast** – the characters in a play and the actors who play them
>
> **director** – the person who is in charge of how the actors perform, how the set is built, and so on
>
> **props** – objects the actors use in the play, such as newspapers, dishes, or swords
>
> **set** – the stage and scenery used in a play
>
> **stage** – a raised floor on which actors move and speak
>
> **theater** – a building with a stage and seats for the audience

CCS: RL.4.5

 TIP 11: **The dialogue and actions in a play are very important.**

Remember, plays don't use details the way prose does. The characters' dialogue and actions tell the audience about the characters. It also helps the audience follow the plot.

 TIP 12: **Stage directions give information about the actors and the set.**

Stage directions tell how and where the actors should move on the stage. They also tell how the set should look. Playwrights use stage directions to give information about things such as lighting and set changes. They also use stage directions to tell how an actor should say a certain line. These directions are usually placed inside parentheses ( ) and printed in *italic* type.

Here is a script for the first scene of a play about the great hero Hercules.

Hercules and the Apples of Zeus

a Greek myth

adapted for the stage by Red Gomez

CAST OF CHARACTERS

THE PROFESSOR, a narrator

HERCULES, a mythical Greek hero

ATLAS, Titan giant who carries the world on his back

**ACT ONE,
SCENE ONE**

SETTING: *A bare stage, except for a speaker's stand from which THE PROFESSOR speaks. A spotlight shines on THE PROFESSOR. Stage lights come up showing HERCULES on his journey, carrying a long walking stick.*

PROFESSOR: Hercules was perhaps the greatest hero in Greek mythology. He was sentenced by the god Apollo to serve a king for twelve years.

As part of that sentence, Hercules had to perform twelve superhuman feats. His journey and suffering earned him everlasting fame. After eight years, his eleventh dangerous challenge was to steal golden apples from the garden of Zeus. To do this, he needed help from Atlas, a strong Titan giant. Here we see Hercules beginning his journey.

(Stage lights come up. HERCULES moves about the stage slowly, as if on guard. He comes upon ATLAS, who is stooped over and carries a huge globe on his shoulders.)

HERCULES: Atlas, I will carry your load if you will do me a favor.

ATLAS: Anything, Hercules, if you will carry my heavy burden. I would be most thankful.

HERCULES: Can you bring me Zeus's golden apples? I must gather them if I am to survive.

ATLAS: I will gladly help you, Hercules.

(HERCULES takes the globe, and ATLAS disappears into darkness.)

HERCULES: Such a burden bears heavy on the soul as well as on the back. How has Atlas carried this load all these years?

(Stage lights dim to darkness and come back up. Enter ATLAS, carrying the apples.)

ATLAS: These were easy to get, compared to carrying the world on my back. Tell you what, Hercules; I will take these apples to those who threaten you.

HERCULES: Do that, Atlas. But first, can you hold my burden as I change positions? I am afraid the weight affects my legs as well as my back.

(ATLAS puts the apples down and takes the globe. HERCULES picks up the apples.)

HERCULES: Sorry, Atlas. I will be back another time. I will not forget the favor you have done me. *(HERCULES exits running.)*

(Stage lights dim, except for a spotlight on THE PROFESSOR.)

PROFESSOR: Hercules had one more feat to perform before he went down in the record books as the greatest hero in Greek mythology. And that, my friends, will be the subject of our next class.

(Curtain)

14. In the script, what do the stage directions usually tell?

   A. which character is speaking

   B. the words a character speaks

   C. how a character should act

   D. the main setting of the scene

You have learned that there are important differences between prose, poetry, and drama. Writers of prose give readers information using sentences and paragraphs. Poets use words in lines and stanzas to paint pictures in a reader's mind. Drama is written to be performed. It uses dialogue and stage directions. Look for the unique elements in the texts you read. It will help you determine which type of text you are reading.

Lesson Practice begins on the following page.

Directions: The following passages are about a girl who meets twins while traveling. Read the passages, then answer Numbers 1 through 8.

Tweedledum and Tweedledee

by Lewis Carroll

adapted for the stage by Gordon Mertz

CAST OF CHARACTERS

ALICE, a young girl   TWEEDLEDUM, a strange little man

TWEEDLEDEE, his equally strange twin

ACT ONE,
SCENE ONE

SETTING: A dark woods as evening approaches. Tweedledum and Tweedledee stand under a tree, each with an arm around the other. They stand so still that they look like statues.

DUM: *(To Alice)* If you think we're statues, you ought to pay. Art is not made to be looked at for free! No-how!

DEE: *(Tweedledum and Tweedledee exchange sides and replace their arms around each other.)* Contrariwise, meaning "on the other hand," if you think we're alive, you ought to talk to us.

ALICE: *(Looking confused and a bit afraid)* Very sorry, I'm sure.

DUM: *(Angrily)* I know what you're thinking about, but it isn't so, no-how.

DEE: Contrariwise on the other hand, if it was so, it might be; and if it were so, it would be; but as it isn't, it ain't. That's just good sense.

ALICE: *(Becoming anxious and worried)* Which is the best way out of this wood? It's getting so dark. Would you tell me, please? *(Tweedledee and Tweedledum look at each other and grin.*

DUM: The first thing to do when you visit someone is to say "How do you do?" and shake hands.

(The brothers give each other a tight hug and hold out their free hands to shake Alice's.)

ALICE: I don't want to shake hands with either of you first, for fear of hurting the other one's feelings. *(She takes hold of both their hands at once, and the twins whirl Alice around in a circle singing "Here We Go Round the Mulberry Bush.")*

DUM: *(Gasping for breath)* Four times round is enough for one dance! *(They suddenly stop dancing.)*

ALICE: I think it's too late to say "How do you do?" now. We seem to have gotten beyond that! But please, PLEASE. Would you tell me which road leads out of these woods? It's getting dark. I think there must be a thunderstorm coming. *(Sound of wind roaring and whistling)* What a thick, black cloud that is. Do you think it's going to rain?

(Tweedledum opens a large umbrella over himself and his brother, then looks up into it.)

DUM: I don't think so, at least not under *here*. No-how!

ALICE: But it may rain *outside*.

DEE: It may—if it chooses. We don't care, contrariwise.

DUM: *(Pointing to the sky)* That's not a cloud. It's a large crow!

(The twins run into the woods, screaming. Alice runs into the woods in the opposite direction and stops under a large tree.)

ALICE: That's no crow. It has no wings. That's a storm cloud, and it's stirring up quite a wind in these woods. Look, here's somebody's blanket being blown away. I'll use it to protect myself from the rain. Now, where did those strange little men go? They have been no help at all.

(Curtain)

Tweedledum and Tweedledee

adapted from *Through the Looking-Glass*

by Lewis Carroll

They were standing under a tree, each with an arm round the other's neck. Alice knew which was which in a moment, because one of them had "DUM" sewn on his collar, and the other "DEE."

"I suppose they've each got 'TWEEDLE' round at the back of the collar," she said to herself.

They stood so still that she quite forgot they were alive. She was just looking round to see if "TWEEDLE" was written at the back when she was startled by a voice coming from the one marked "DUM."

"If you think we're statues," he said, "you ought to pay, you know. Art wasn't made to be looked at for nothing, no-how!"

"Contrariwise," added Dee, "if you think we're alive, you ought to speak."

"I'm sure I'm very sorry," was all Alice could say. The words of the old song kept ringing through her head like the ticking of a clock:

> *"Tweedledum and Tweedledee*
> *Agreed to have a battle;*
> *For Tweedledum said Tweedledee*
> *Had spoiled his nice new rattle.*
>
> *Just then flew down a monstrous crow,*
> *As black as a tar-barrel;*
> *Which frightened both the heroes so,*
> *They quite forgot their quarrel."*

"I know what you're thinking about," said Tweedledum, "but it isn't so, no-how."

"Contrariwise," continued Tweedledee, "if it was so, it might be; and if it were so, it would be; but as it isn't, it ain't. That's just good sense."

"I was thinking," Alice said very politely, "which is the best way out of this wood? It's getting so dark. Would you tell me, please?"

But the little men only looked at each other and grinned.

Alice pointed her finger at Tweedledum so they would know who was to answer.

"You've been wrong!" cried Tweedledum. "The first thing in a visit is to say 'How do you do?' and shake hands!" And here the two brothers gave each other a hug. Then they held out the two hands that were free to shake hands with her.

Alice did not want to shake hands with either of them first, for fear of hurting the other one's feelings. So she took hold of both hands at once. The next moment they were dancing round in a ring. This seemed quite natural, and she was not even surprised to hear music playing. It seemed to come from the tree under which they were dancing.

She did find it funny to find herself singing "Here We Go Round the Mulberry Bush." She didn't know when she began, but somehow it felt as if she'd been singing it a long, long time!

The other two dancers were very soon out of breath. "Four times round is enough for one dance," Tweedledum panted out. They left off dancing as suddenly as they had begun. The music stopped at the same moment.

Then they let go of Alice's hands and stood looking at her for a minute. There was an awkward pause. Alice didn't know how to begin talking with people she had just been dancing with. "It would never do to say 'How do you do?' now," she said. "We seem to have got beyond that, somehow! But, please, would you tell me which road leads out of the wood? I'd better be going, for really it's coming on very dark. Do you think it's going to rain?"

Tweedledum spread a large umbrella over himself and his brother, and looked up into it. "No, I don't think it is," he said, "at least—not under *here*. No-how."

"But it may rain *outside*?"

"It may—if it chooses," said Tweedledee. "We've no objection. Contrariwise."

It was getting dark so suddenly that Alice thought there must be a thunderstorm coming on. "What a thick black cloud that is!" she said. "And how fast it comes! Why, I do believe it's got wings!"

"It's the crow!" Tweedledum cried out in a shrill voice of alarm, and the two brothers took to their heels and were out of sight in a moment.

Alice ran a little way into the wood and stopped under a large tree. "It can never get at me *here*," she thought. "It's far too large to squeeze itself in among the trees. But I wish it wouldn't flap its wings so—it makes quite a hurricane in the wood—here's somebody's shawl being blown away!"

1. **In the play, what is the scene <u>mostly</u> about?**

   A. Strange twins show Alice the path out of the woods.

   B. Alice meets twins who speak mostly in nonsense.

   C. Alice and her friends sing and dance when they meet.

   D. A storm forces Alice to hide in the woods with strangers.

2. **How does the playwright show what Alice is thinking?**

   _____

   _____

3. **Which word <u>best</u> tells about Alice?**

   A. angry

   B. patient

   C. startled

   D. unusual

4. **In both the play and the story, Alice and the twins dance and sing. Explain how each passage tells about this.**

   _____

   _____

   _____

   _____

5. The story contains a song about Tweedledee and Tweedledum. Which of the following <u>best</u> tells about the song's rhyme pattern?

    A. Every line of each stanza rhymes.

    B. Every other line of each stanza rhymes.

    C. Odd lines rhyme, and even lines rhyme.

    D. Each pair of lines in a stanza rhyme.

6. How is the setting described in both the play and in the story?

    _____

    _____

7. Why do Tweedledum and Tweedledee run into the woods?

    A. They fear the crow from the song.

    B. They want to get out of the storm.

    C. They are trying to confuse Alice.

    D. They are showing Alice the way out.

8. Read this sentence from the play.

    "I'll use it to protect myself from the rain."

    What does *protect* mean?

    _____

    _____

Lesson 6: Story Elements

When a writer tells a made-up story, it is called **fiction**. But writing fiction isn't just making things up. In this lesson, you will learn how stories work using characters, setting, and plot.

Character and Setting

All made-up stories have characters and setting. **Characters** are the people or animals that take part in a story. **Setting** is where and when a story happens. The following tips help you find details about characters and setting in the plays and stories you read.

TIP 1: Look for details about the characters.

Authors often tell what their characters look like, but that is not all you need to know about them. Watch for what characters say and do. You can also learn from characters' thoughts. Notice how they act toward others. Think about how they might act differently around different people. What do they do when they are alone? All these details add up to tell you what each character is like.

You can also learn about the characters in a drama this way. The dialogue and stage directions in a play show you what the characters say and do.

The writer of a story can't just tell you everything you need to know. So you must use clues the writer gives that tell about what characters look like and how they act.

Read the following passage, and then answer Numbers 1 through 5.

> Kelly marched across the playground toward Junior Becker. She was the smallest student in her class, but she seemed about as big as a thunderstorm at that moment. Just the look in her dark brown eyes would've been enough to knock most kids over. She'd rolled up the sleeves of her baggy black sweatshirt and was pulling her little brother Ben behind her. Ben was still wiping the mashed peanut butter and jelly sandwich from his blond hair. Kelly's friends—Mara, Shelley, and Alisha—were there, too, running behind her, telling her to forget about it.
>
> "Not until Junior apologizes," Kelly said.
>
> Just ahead, by the Dumpster, stood Junior. He was as thick as a tree trunk and surrounded by his goofy friends.

CCS: RL.4.3

1. Give two details that describe what Kelly looks like.

_____

_____

2. Write a sentence that tells what kind of person Kelly is.

_____

_____

3. Give two details that describe Junior Becker.

_____

_____

4. Based on the information in the passage, which of the following best describes Ben?

    A. tall
    B. strong
    C. blond
    D. brown-eyed

5. What probably happened between Junior and Ben before the passage started?

_____

_____

_____

_____

Character Clues

Here are some questions to ask yourself about the main character in a story:

- What is the character like?

- What does the character want most? Why?

- What is keeping the character from getting what he or she wants?

- How will the character solve the problem?

- Does the character change during the story? How?

- Would the character really do this? Do his or her actions make sense? Why or why not?

TIP 2: Think about who is telling the story.

The **narrator** is the person telling the story. Sometimes the narrator is a character in the story. Other times, the narrator is outside of the story.

Point of view tells whether a narrator is inside the story or outside the story. A **first-person narrator** is a character in the story. This kind of narrator can tell you what he or she is thinking and feeling. But this narrator can't tell you what other characters are feeling or thinking. A first-person narrator uses words like *I, we, our,* and so on.

A **third-person narrator** is not a character in the story. This narrator can often tell you what many of the characters are thinking and feeling. A third-person narrator uses words like *he, she, they,* and so on.

6. Read the following sentences from *Otherwise Known as Sheila the Great* by Judy Blume. Circle the words that show the reader that this story has a first-person narrator.

   Today was so hot! My clothes stuck to me, and my brain felt all tired out.

Read the following paragraph from *Homer Price* by Robert McCloskey.

   About two miles outside of Centerburg, where Route 56 meets Route 56A, there lives a boy named Homer. Homer's father owns a tourist camp. Homer's mother cooks fried chicken and hamburgers in the lunchroom and takes care of the tourist cabins while his father takes care of the filling station. Homer does odd jobs about the place.

7. Which point of view is *Homer Price* told from?

   _____

8. Who is telling the story?

   A. Homer

   B. Homer's father

   C. Homer's mother

   D. an outside narrator

CCS: RL.4.3

TIP 3: **Look for details that tell you where and when the story takes place.**

Details that describe the setting will help you understand the story. The author will create a picture of it in your mind in a few ways. First, the narrator will tell about the place and time in which story happens. You may also learn about the setting from the characters. They may talk about where they are or where they're going. Other details may come from characters' thoughts.

There is more to setting than place, of course. Notice the season, the time of day, and the weather. Does the story happen in the past or the future? In the real world or a magical land? Each of these setting details has an effect on the story.

In a drama, of course, the writer does not tell you about the setting. But playwrights have many tricks for bringing the setting to life. The set itself should give you some idea of where the story takes place. It may be outside a castle, deep in the forest, or inside a house. Sound effects can create wind or rain. Characters' costumes can show time, place, and season, too. And, of course, the characters themselves may discuss where they are.

The paragraph that follows has been adapted from *Treasure Island* by Robert Louis Stevenson. Read the paragraph. Then answer Numbers 9 through 11.

It was early on a January morning. The waves brushed softly against the stones of England's shore. The old pirate had woken up earlier than usual. He left the Admiral Benbow Inn and walked toward the beach, looking for a seafaring man with one leg. His sword swung under the flaps of his blue coat. He held a brass telescope and his hat was tilted back upon his head. I remember that his breath looked like smoke in the cold air. And the last sound I heard from him was a snort as he disappeared behind a big rock.

9. Where does the story take place?

_____

_____

_____

10. Describe the weather in the story.

_____

_____

_____

11. What events are taking place during the story?

_____

_____

_____

Plot

A story doesn't really get going until something happens. The **plot** is what happens in a story. The following tips will show you how to find the main problems that characters must face in a story. You will also learn how to follow the important events, tell what will happen next, and understand how the main problems are solved.

TIP 4: Find the problems in the story.

In most stories, the characters have some sort of problem to solve. The story's **conflict** is the problem the characters face. Both plays and stories are based on problems that must be solved.

Problems are an important part of a plot. They get the story going. There may be one or two big problems in the beginning and several smaller problems along the way.

Read the following passage, which has been retold from *Robinson Crusoe* by Daniel Defoe. Then answer Number 12.

> I, Robinson Crusoe, was shipwrecked during a terrible storm. I washed up on the shore of a miserable island. The rest of the ship's company had drowned, and I was nearly dead. At first, I was joyful for having been spared. But I quickly came to realize that I had no way of providing myself food or shelter. I soon discovered that most of the ship remained some distance from shore. I made myself a raft and carried away food, tools, and rifles. Then I began to think about ways to build a shelter.

12. Describe two of Robinson Crusoe's main problems in the passage.

_____

_____

_____

TIP 5: Decide who or what is mixed up in the problem.

The main character of a story or play will always face problems. That's just the way it goes. Sometimes, the problem will be with another character, like a pesky elf, a stern teacher, or a neighborhood bully. Sometimes, the problem will be with a thing, like a broken bicycle chain or a difficult test. And sometimes the problem will be within the character. The character may wonder, *Should I tell my parents that I scratched their new car with my bike? Or should I be quiet and hope they don't find out?*

Read the following paragraph, adapted from *The Monster Who Grew Small* by Joan Grant. Then answer Numbers 13 and 14.

> Far to the South, beyond the Third Waterfall, there was a small village where a certain boy lived with his uncle. Whenever the boy had to go down to the river, he thought that crocodiles would eat him. When he went into the forest, he thought that the shadows hid snakes and that hairy spiders waited under the leaves to pounce on him. The place that always felt especially dangerous was on the path down to the village. Whenever he had to go along it, he used to run.

13. What is the boy's main problem?

    A. He dreams about crocodiles, snakes, and spiders.

    B. He lives in a small village with his uncle.

    C. He fears that wild creatures will attack him.

    D. He can't swim in the river.

14. The boy's main conflict is with

    A. several bullies who live in the next village.

    B. the small village where he lives.

    C. the uncle he lives with.

    D. his fear of the world outside his uncle's home.

TIP 6: Look for the main events.

As you read a story or a play, look for the main events. Remember, the main events are the most important events in the story, the ones that keep the plot moving. As the plot moves on, the conflict, or problem, may get worse. The **climax** is the part of the plot when the characters have to solve the problem.

Take special note of what the characters do. Their actions are often the most important events. You should be able to retell the plot using details about what the characters did, said, and thought.

Read the following passage from *Terror in Touchstone House.* As you read, ask yourself questions such as these: What problems do the characters face? What actions do they take to solve their problems? What are the most important events in the story?

from

Terror in Touchstone House

by Nick Liakouras

Nancy held the flashlight while the twins, Tony and Noreen, crawled along the edge of the dark, spooky room. They moved slowly, feeling among the scattered books that lay about on the dusty floorboards.

"It has to be here—in this old library room," Nancy said bravely. She was the most lion-hearted of the bunch. "Martin heard the man on the bus say that it would be hidden in Touchstone House until tomorrow morning. We have to find it tonight! Someone's bound to come back for it as soon as the sun comes up."

Dry boards squeaked as the children moved slowly across the old, wobbly floor.

"Over here, Nancy," Tony whispered. "Shine the flashlight down here. I think I've found something."

Nancy slid the pool of light across the wooden floor. She gasped as the twins jumped to their feet with strange screams, screams that sounded more like grunts.

CCSs: RL.4.3, RL.4.10

"What is it?" Nancy asked.

"I don't know," Noreen said in a shaky voice. "I don't know. But it has yellow eyes and it crawled into that hole in the floor."

"Let's get out of here," Tony whispered, running his hands along the dark wall, trying to find the door.

They stumbled across the empty library room, and then ran along the dark hallway, down the crumbling front steps, and out into the moonlight.

Stopping in the shadows outside the iron entrance gate, the three detectives were quiet—except for the wild thumping of their hearts.

(*To be continued . . .*)

15. What problem brings the children to the house?

    A. They must find something before morning.

    B. The library room is dusty and covered with old books.

    C. The floor of Touchstone House is old and wobbly.

    D. Something is crawling into a hole in the floor.

16. Why do the children run from the house?

    A. They hear someone coming.

    B. They see something with yellow eyes.

    C. Their flashlight does not work.

    D. The floorboards make squeaky noises.

TIP 7: Notice how the main problem is solved.

The **resolution** of the story is when the problem is finally solved. Pay close attention to how the characters solve their problems. Ask yourself, "How have the characters and their world changed by the end of the story?"

Not all stories have a resolution that answers all your questions. The characters may not live happily ever after. In some stories, the main problem won't be solved. Instead, the main characters may learn something new that helps them live with their problems. And sometimes, the author simply lets you imagine your own ending to a story.

Continue reading the passage.

from

Terror in Touchstone House

(*Continued*)

"Now what?" Nancy asked in a loud whisper.

"I have to think," Tony said. He lowered himself to his knees just as the moon dipped behind a large gray cloud. "Why should we run from a little thing with yellow eyes? We'll have to go back. If we don't get the map first, there's gonna be real trouble."

"Can't we wait until morning?" Noreen wanted to know.

"Get real, Noreen!" Tony snapped. "Do you want somebody to find it before we do?"

"Not really, but that place gives me the creeps," Noreen whispered.

"All right," Nancy said. "Both of you, be calm. We have to try it one more time. Come on. The moon's out again. Quick! Let's run for the door."

They paused, then raced for the entrance steps and the great oak door that led into the crumbling Touchstone House. They stopped just inside, and Tony checked quickly up and down Brookwood Avenue before closing the door.

"There's our friend, Mr. Yellow Eyes," he said, aiming the light at a young gray squirrel. They watched the yellow beam shine in its tiny eyes. The startled animal sat up and stared at the visitors. It then waved goodbye and scurried toward its hole.

"It must have a nest under the floorboards," Nancy said. She bent down and peeked into the hole. Laying inside were tiny shreds of paper and the tattered remains of an old drawing. "It looks like Mr. Yellow Eyes has found the perfect material to line his nest," she said.

Tony shined the light onto the worn paper. "It's the map," he said, snatching it breathlessly. In places, whole chunks had been eaten away.

Far below them, the great door to Touchstone House squeaked open, and then closed with a thundering boom.

17. How did the children solve the problem of finding the map?

    A. They found it in a squirrel's nest.

    B. They gave up looking for it.

    C. They got their parents to help them.

    D. They found it on the stairs.

18. What new problem do the children have at the end of the passage?

    A. Mr. Yellow Eyes has run away with the map.

    B. Someone else may have entered the house.

    C. Nothing is left of the map, so they must find another.

    D. The man from the bus finds the map before they do.

TIP 8: Use illustrations to follow the plot and see the changes in characters and the setting.

When you read a comic book, pictures tell the story. They show all the events of the plot. When you read a story, words do that job. Illustrations can help.

Many stories include illustrations. **Illustrations** are pictures of what happens in the story. They also show the characters and setting. They do not show things that are not in the story. Instead, they make sure readers understand what is written.

Few stories show pictures of the whole plot. But some include pictures of the major events. When you read, look back at the pictures. They will quickly remind you of what happened earlier. Pictures can also help you understand what is happening. If you do not understand events in the plot, look at a picture for clues.

Illustrations often show changes in character or setting. The pictures may show that winter has turned to spring. Or they may show that people have grown older.

Imagine you are reading a story about a knight and a princess. The knight wears shiny armor. The princess is dressed in a beautiful gown. The characters soon have a run-in with a cranky dragon. Afterward, the knight's armor is dented and dirty. The princess's gown is torn and burnt. Her long hair has become tangled and wild.

The pictures that appear with the text will be sure to show these changes. They help you see and remember what has happened in the story.

Note: You should *not* look at the pictures instead of reading. Pictures can help you understand what you read, but they can't take the place of the text.

Look at these pictures from the fairy tale "Beauty and the Beast." Then answer Numbers 19 and 20.

19. What has changed from the first picture to the second? Name at least two differences.

_____

_____

_____

_____

20. What important event from the plot of "Beauty and the Beast" is shown in the first picture?

    A. The Beast falls in love with Beauty.

    B. Beauty at first fears the grouchy Beast.

    C. Beauty falls in love with the Beast.

    D. A magic spell turned a prince into the Beast.

CCS: RL.4.7

 TIP 9: Listen closely to plays and stories read aloud.

Another way to understand a story or play is to listen to it. For instance, dramas are performed by actors. You can learn a lot about their characters from how they speak. Two different characters might say the same words, but in their own way.

Think about the sentence "I love you." It can be said in thousands of ways and mean different things. The meaning depends on what the speaker wants. Is the character a child trying to get out of trouble? Or is she an older woman saying goodbye to the house she grew up in? The way the actor says the words can give you clues that reading them might not.

Lesson Practice begins on the following page.

Directions: This passage is about a boy who ruins his bike and needs some help. Read the passage. Then answer Numbers 1 through 8.

Mr. Rodriguez and the Bicycle

by Maria Sosa

Manuel had nobody to blame but himself. Nobody!

Grandma had told him, "Manuel, when you get home from school, lean your bike up against a tree. Don't lay it on the ground, or on the sidewalk, or in the driveway." Why hadn't he listened to his grandmother? He knew why.

He had been in a hurry yesterday evening. He and his friends had been playing baseball when he should have been home doing his chores.

Almost everyone in his family was now at work. Only Manuel and Grandma were left at home, and she had told him, "Manuel, I'm going to need your help this afternoon."

But there he was, on second base with the score tied. The sun was setting. Rocky Garcia was at bat. Rocky hit a grounder between shortstop and third base, and Manuel ran for home like he had a V-8 engine under his feet. They had won!

After the game, he raced home on his bike, which he called Fabulous Freddy. When Manuel was on Freddy, he felt like a superhero out to save the planet. He flew home, hoping Grandma wouldn't notice that he had failed to do his afternoon chores.

That's how it happened, a very sad Manuel told himself. He had scored the winning run, but he had also disappointed Grandma. He was in such a hurry that he left his bike lying in the driveway. Now somebody in the apartment building had driven over his bike. If Grandma found out about this, she'd be more disappointed and doubly mad.

What am I going to do now? thought Manuel. He didn't have any money to fix the bike. Grandma would surely find out. And now he couldn't ride around feeling like a superhero. Poor Manuel. It just wasn't right, even if it was his fault.

Across the street, old Mr. Rodriguez saw the sad boy and knew what had happened. Mr. Rodriguez saw everything that happened in the neighborhood. He even saw Mrs. Lee drive her pickup truck over the bike. It wasn't Mrs. Lee's fault. She didn't know it was there. And Mr. Rodriguez couldn't even fault Manuel. Could the boy help it if he was young and foolish?

"Say, Manuel, why so unhappy?" Mr. Rodriguez asked.

Manuel didn't answer. Like most of the young people in the neighborhood, he didn't much like Mr. Rodriguez. It seemed that all he did was sit on his front porch and spy on his neighbors. What the young people didn't know was that for over twenty years Mr. Rodriguez had worked as hard as anybody. He worked until his back became so painful that he could hardly walk.

"Somebody drove over your bike, eh?" Mr. Rodriguez asked. He was still sitting on the front porch, trying to get Manuel to speak up.

"Uh-huh," said Manuel, nodding his head. He didn't look up, and he wanted to say, "Mind your own business, old man." But he didn't, because he knew that if Grandma heard him, he'd really be in trouble.

"I think I know what you need, young man." And with that, Mr. Rodriguez got up and left his porch.

Manuel watched as the old man went around his driveway to a run-down garage that looked as though it could tumble to the ground at any minute. Mr. Rodriguez walked with the aid of a cane, and he looked very old, even though he was about the same age as Manuel's grandma.

"Over here, Manuel, and bring your bike."

Manuel got up and slowly crossed the street. He approached the entrance to Mr. Rodriguez's garage. There, among heaps of junk and dust, Manuel saw several bicycles leaning against the back wall. Mr. Rodriguez had found one, and using a wrench, he was taking off the front wheel. "This one will fit your bicycle," the old man said. "Let me help you change the wheel."

An hour later, Manuel was flying down the back streets of town. Off in the distance, he thought he could hear the sounds of thunder. But Manuel paid it no mind. He was out to save the planet. He was soaring through space and time on his bicycle. He was a superhero, protecting humankind—including his friend Mr. Rodriguez—from atop a speeding bicycle named Fabulous Freddy.

1. **What is Manuel's <u>main</u> problem in the passage?**

    A. He wants Mr. Rodriguez to leave him alone.

    B. He wants to win the neighborhood baseball game.

    C. He wants to pretend he is a superhero while riding his bike.

    D. He wants to keep Grandma from learning his bike was run over.

2. **Where does <u>most</u> of the passage take place?**

    _____

    _____

3. **Who is the speaker in the passage?**

    A. Manuel

    B. Mr. Rodriguez

    C. Grandma

    D. an outside narrator

4. **List two details that describe Mr. Rodriguez.**

    _____

    _____

    _____

5. **Which of these events happens first in the passage?**

    A. Manuel scores the winning run.

    B. Mr. Rodriguez fixes Manuel's bicycle.

    C. Someone drives over Manuel's bicycle.

    D. Manuel leaves his bicycle on the ground.

6. **What change is shown by the two illustrations?**

    _____

    _____

7. **How do Manuel's feelings toward Mr. Rodriguez change?**

    A. Manuel begins to like Mr. Rodriguez.

    B. Manuel becomes angry with Mr. Rodriguez.

    C. Manuel gets disappointed by Mr. Rodriguez.

    D. Manuel starts to find Mr. Rodriguez nosy.

8. **According to the passage, Mr. Rodriguez has a "run-down garage." What does** *run-down* **mean?**

    _____

    _____

CCS: L.4.5a

Lesson 7: Literary Devices

Imagine that a friend writes a paper about a winter weekend at a cabin in the mountains. It starts like this:

> I was a million miles away from school, homework, and my paper route! The world was a frosted wedding cake. From the large front window, the snow looked like marshmallow topping. Inside the cabin, a great fire licked at a steaming kettle of spicy apple cider.

Your friend uses special language to tell readers about his family's winter weekend trip. Using **figurative language** is a way that authors compare ideas to help readers imagine what they are reading. There are several kinds of figurative language in this paragraph, including metaphor and simile.

Authors have some other items in their bag of tricks. They use wise or clever sayings. They mention ideas from famous stories. You'll have more fun reading when you know some of the games that authors play with words.

TIP 1: Authors compare things using similes and metaphors.

Figurative language can be used in poetry, drama, and prose. The most common forms are simile and metaphor. Remember, **similes** compare two things by using the word *like* or the word *as*.

> Katy is <u>as</u> pretty <u>as</u> a picture.

> The road lay before us <u>like</u> a ribbon of concrete.

Metaphors compare two things by making one thing into another. Authors don't say something is *like* something else. They say or hint that one thing *is* another.

> The wheat field was a golden sea that stretched to the horizon. (A wheat field is called a sea.)

> Edgar plowed through his math problems. (Doing homework is likened to plowing.)

Read these lines from a poem, then answer Numbers 1 and 2.

> The moon is a bone-white sailing ship
> Skimming an ink-black sea.

1. These lines contain examples of

    A. simile.

    B. metaphor.

    C. prose.

    D. rhyme.

CCS: L.4.5b

2. In these lines, what things does the speaker compare?

_____

_____

 TIP 2: Idioms don't mean exactly what they say.

An **idiom** is figurative language that has become a common saying. "All bark and no bite" is an example of an idiom. It means that someone is loud but harmless. Like other idioms, it doesn't mean exactly what it says. That's the fun of using idioms.

Here are some more examples of idioms.

Idiom	What It Means
costs an arm and a leg	is expensive
backseat driver	someone who gives unwanted advice or directions
cross your fingers	hope for the best
everything but the kitchen sink	almost everything

Read the following sentences. Then write the meaning of each underlined idiom on the line provided.

3. Keesha was about to leave when her dad called out, "Hold your horses—you forgot your lunch."

_____

4. Marta thought learning to juggle would be hard, but it was a piece of cake.

_____

 TIP 3: Proverbs and adages are common sayings.

A **proverb** is a wise saying. It is short and easy to remember. Like an idiom, it does not mean exactly what it says. It uses figurative language to make its point. An **adage** is an old proverb that is well known. Some adages and their meanings follow.

CCS: L.4.5b

Adage	What It Means
Don't look a gift horse in the mouth.	Don't complain about things you are given.
Look before you leap.	Think about what might happen before you do something.
A stitch in time saves nine.	Fixing a slight problem can stop it from growing worse.
Where there's smoke, there's fire.	If there are signs of a problem, there probably is one.

You can explain proverbs and adages yourself. First, try to understand its message. What simple truth can you draw from it? This idea should be true of life in general, not just the moment the proverb describes.

For example, think about the adage "don't look a gift horse in the mouth." Looking into a horse's mouth is a way of making sure it is healthy. Imagine you were given a horse. If you were to examine it, you would be showing that you don't trust the person who gave it to you. The adage means you should be thankful for gifts. Don't question them or point out problems with them.

5. Which of the following best explains what this proverb means?

    The grass is always greener on the other side of the fence.

    A. If you take good care of your lawn, you will be happy.
    B. It's easy to think other people have better lives than ours.
    C. The best way to get things done is to do them yourself.
    D. The farther away things are, the better they look.

TIP 4: Some words and phrases come from myths.

Myths are ancient stories about gods and heroes. They often try to explain things in nature. For example, one myth says that Prometheus stole the secret of fire from the gods. He taught human beings how to make fire.

Many words come from the names in myths. Authors use these words to compare things in their stories to the myths. An author might write this sentence:

For Hassan, cleaning his room was a Sisyphean chore.

CCS: RL.4.4

Sisyphean is one of the more difficult words you might encounter in your reading. However, you can understand this sentence if you know the myth of Sisyphus. He was a king who angered the gods. To punish him, they made him push a heavy rock up a steep hill. Just as he reached the top, the rock would roll back down. Sisyphus had to push the rock, over and over, forever.

Now that you know the story of Sisyphus, you probably have a better understanding of what a "Sisyphean chore" is. Hassan feels like cleaning his room is a job that never ends.

Here are a few more characters from myths that you should know:

- **Hercules** was the strongest man in the world. To make up for his bad deeds, he did twelve jobs called labors. These were good works that only he was strong enough to do. For one labor, Hercules cleaned a giant cattle stable by changing a river's flow.

- **Pandora** was a woman who opened a box to see what was inside. She let out all of the evils of the world. Pandora's simple act had terrible effects she didn't expect.

- **Achilles** was a great warrior. When he was a baby, his mother dipped him in a magical river. Wherever the water touched him, he could not be harmed. But his mother held him by the heel, so his heel was his one weakness. Achilles was defeated when an enemy struck his heel.

- **Odysseus** was a Greek king who went to war against the Trojans. During the war, he hid his men inside a large wooden horse. Then he gave the horse to the Trojans as a gift. The Trojans brought the horse inside the city walls. That night, the Greeks attacked. *The Odyssey* is the story of Odysseus' long journey home after the war.

Read these sentences. Then answer Number 6.

> Kimiyo had only wanted to learn how her computer worked. But now there were parts all over the table. She felt like she had opened <u>Pandora's box</u>.

6. What does the author mean by saying Kimiyo "felt like she had opened Pandora's box"?

   A. Kimiyo has done something truly evil.

   B. Kimiyo has opened a box to see what's inside.

   C. Kimiyo did not expect so many problems.

   D. Kimiyo is being punished by the gods.

Lesson Practice begins on the following page.

Directions: This passage is about a new girl with a lot of talent. Read the passage. Then answer Numbers 1 through 8.

The New Girl

The class was gathered around Lauren's desk before the morning bell.

"Show us the race car, Lauren!" Travis begged.

"No!" Regina said, stepping in front of Travis. "The unicorn!"

Lauren smiled and flipped through her sketchbook. She was eating this up. Everyone loved her drawings. Sometimes her teacher, Mrs. Cordova, even let her draw pictures on the board.

The bell rang, and the students found their seats. Mrs. Cordova walked in with a girl nobody had seen before.

"Class," Mrs. Cordova said. "I want to introduce Nell Williams. Nell just moved here from Georgia. She tells me that she loves to draw."

Lauren smiled to herself. If Nell thought she was a great artist, she had another thing coming.

Nell took a sketchbook out of her bag. She showed a few pages to the class. Lauren couldn't believe what she saw. Nell had drawn the most beautiful pictures. The class was amazed.

"Those are better than Lauren's drawings!" Travis said.

Mrs. Cordova hushed Travis and turned to Nell. "Lauren is also an artist, Nell. Maybe Lauren can tell you about the contest coming up."

Lauren felt like she had been hit by a truck. Every year, the school held a contest to see who could draw the best design for the yearbook's cover. Lauren had never won, but she felt this was her year. Now she saw her chances going up in smoke.

Days passed. The class now gathered around Nell's desk each morning before the bell. Lauren felt sick as she listened to everyone "ooh" and "ahh" over Nell's work.

"I don't know why my mom's making me enter this contest," Travis said one morning. "Nell's going to win. Everyone knows that!" The class agreed.

Lauren wanted to cry. For days she had been trying to draw an eagle soaring proudly above the school. It was their mascot, and Lauren knew it had to be just right. But it looked terrible. She could draw horses, tigers, people, and dogs. But for some reason, birds were her Achilles' heel. She decided to give up.

"Mrs. Cordova?" Lauren said one afternoon after everyone had left. "I'm not going to enter the contest this year."

"Why not?" Mrs. Cordova said.

"I'm not good at art anymore."

Mrs. Cordova frowned. "I'm going to take a shot in the dark. This wouldn't have anything to do with Nell, would it?"

Lauren didn't answer.

"Oh, Lauren," Mrs. Cordova said. "You're going to meet a lot of people with a lot of talents. Some won't be as good as you. Some will be better. But you must never forget that your talent is yours and nobody else's."

Lauren felt confused.

"Let me ask you this," Mrs. Cordova said. "Do you draw for Nell, Travis, or me?"

Lauren shook her head.

"You draw for yourself, Lauren. Your talent belongs to you. And if you don't enter that contest, the only person you'll hurt is yourself."

Lauren understood now. She had a picture to finish.

A week later, the results were in. Lauren felt good. Her drawing had turned out great—the best she'd ever done. Nell had turned in a great picture, too. Before Mrs. Cordova announced the winner, Lauren leaned over to Nell.

"I loved your picture," Lauren said. "Good luck."

Mrs. Cordova said, "The results are in, and I'm proud to say that the winner is from this class. Congratulations to Travis Nguyen!" Mrs. Cordova said, uncovering the entry. Both girls' mouths dropped. On a poster board, Travis had written the words "EAGLES ROCK!" in colorful, bubbly letters.

Lauren and Nell rolled their eyes and laughed. Suddenly, the contest seemed like the least important thing in the world.

1. **Which of these sentences from the passage is a simile?**

   A. "The class was gathered around Lauren's desk before the morning bell."

   B. "Nell took a sketchbook out of her bag."

   C. "Lauren couldn't believe what she saw."

   D. "Lauren felt like she had been hit by a truck."

2. **Read the following sentences from the passage.**

   "She could draw horses, tigers, people, and dogs. But for some reason, birds were her Achilles' heel."

   What does *Achilles' heel* <u>most likely</u> mean?

   _____

   _____

3. **Read the following sentences from the passage.**

   "Lauren smiled and flipped through her sketchbook. She was eating this up."

   What does *eating this up* mean?

   A. enjoying herself

   B. having a snack

   C. growing bored

   D. feeling nervous

4. **According to the passage, if Nell thought she was a good artist, "she had another thing coming." What does this phrase <u>most likely</u> mean?**

   _____

   _____

5. Mrs. Cordova says, "I'm going to take a shot in the dark." What does *take a shot in the dark* mean?

   A. try something hard

   B. make a wild guess

   C. take a photograph

   D. feel disappointment

6. Read the following sentence from the passage.

   "Now she saw her chances going up in smoke."

   What does this sentence mean?

   _____

   _____

7. Where does this passage take place?

   A. at Lauren's house

   B. on the playground

   C. in Mrs. Cordova's classroom

   D. in the school hallway

8. What is Lauren's <u>main</u> problem, and how is it solved?

   _____

   _____

   _____

   _____

Lesson 8: Informational Text

When you read a story or an article, you judge its quality. **Quality** is how good something is. Can you trust the information in it? Is it true and correct? Does the writer give reasons and evidence to back up his or her ideas? This lesson will give you some tips to help you answer these questions.

Read the following letter. It was written in response to a school newspaper article titled "Should Students Use Calculators?"

Letter to the Editor

Dear Editor:

I think we should be allowed to use calculators in school. Calculators are used every day all over the world. Like computers, they are important tools that we should learn how to use.

Some people say calculators keep us from learning how to do things like addition and multiplication in our minds. Here is my idea: Allow us to use calculators only on tests. We would get plenty of practice doing math problems the long way on our homework. On test day, we would spend less time writing to figure out the answers. The time we save could be spent answering even more problems. Jefferson Primary School lets students use calculators on tests, and their test scores have gone up 20 percent in the last year!

In addition, because we would write less, our papers wouldn't be as messy. Teachers could grade them faster and more easily. We would use less paper on tests, and that's the only way to help the environment. Also, my hand would be a lot less tired at the end of the day.

I hope your readers will think about these ideas.

Sincerely,

David Wilson

David Wilson

TIP 1: Decide how the author's choices show his or her purpose for writing.

Authors write nonfiction for a few reasons. Sometimes the purpose is to inform. To **inform** is to give information. Articles that inform are usually full of **facts**, which are statements that can be proved true. They include few **opinions**, or the author's feeling about the topic. (You'll learn more about fact and opinion later in this lesson.) If there are two sides to an issue, the writer presents each side fairly.

Sometimes the purpose is to persuade. To **persuade** is to make someone agree with an opinion. These articles use facts to support the writer's views. If there are two sides to an issue, the writer presents one as the best.

For example, imagine an article that informs about bears. It lists a number of facts. It explains what bears eat, how big they are, and so on.

Now imagine a writer wants to persuade people to save bears. This article uses different information. It explains how cities have driven bears from their homes. It tells about groups that try to save bears. It also includes opinions about the beauty of the bears.

When trying to decide an author's purpose, look at how the information that author uses helps show why he or she is writing.

1. What kind of information does David Wilson use in his letter?

   A. how calculators work

   B. why calculators are helpful

   C. groups that make calculators

   D. the history of calculators

TIP 2: Decide whether the author supports his or her ideas.

Authors should back up their ideas with evidence to show their ideas are correct. **Evidence** is information that supports an idea. It includes details, examples, and facts. **Facts** are pieces of information that can be proved true or false. Supporting evidence should be clearly linked to the topic.

Writers should also offer reasons to agree with their views. They must explain why readers should accept one view and not another. They should show why something is important. They should tell how following their suggestions will help.

2. Which evidence from David Wilson's letter offers the best support for allowing calculators to be used in schools?

_____

_____

_____

3. Why is this evidence the best support?

_____

_____

_____

 TIP 3: Notice whether a statement is a fact or an opinion.

Ask yourself how the author supports his or her ideas. Is the author making statements of fact or opinion?

As you know, a fact is a statement that can be checked to see if it is true. It uses words with meanings everyone can agree on, such as number or size.

That tree is a yellow poplar. It is a hundred feet tall.

An opinion tells how someone feels. It cannot be checked to see whether it is true. It may be true to some people, but not to others. Opinions use words that mean different things to different people.

The tree in my yard is the most beautiful in town. It has lovely blossoms.

4. Find a statement of fact from David Wilson's letter, and write it on the lines that follow.

_____

_____

_____

5. Find a statement of opinion from David Wilson's letter, and write it on the lines that follow.

_____

_____

_____

Of course, facts can be wrong. For example, an article might contain this fact:

It is 300 miles from London to Paris.

This fact is not correct, but it is still a fact. It uses fact words and can be checked.

You could use an atlas or a Web site to check the distance between London and Paris. (The actual distance between London and Paris is approximately 210 miles, and that is a true fact!)

 ## TIP 4: Check the author's reasoning.

When writers try to persuade the reader, they may make mistakes in their reasoning. In other words, they may use arguments that don't make perfect sense. Here are two common mistakes:

- **slippery slope** – saying that one event will lead to worse and worse events.

  If we start using a different brand of computers, this school will fall apart.

- **false choice** – saying there are only two choices when there are actually more.

  If we can't go to the pool today, there won't be anything to do.

6. Find a mistake in David Wilson's reasoning, and write it on the lines below. Then label it as either a false choice or a slippery slope.

_____

_____

_____

TIP 5: Look at how authors order their ideas.

Understanding how authors organize their writing will help you better understand their ideas. To **organize** means to put ideas in an order that makes sense. Here are some ways authors organize their writing.

- **cause and effect** – explaining how one event causes something else to happen. A writer might use cause and effect to explain night and day.

- **opinion and supporting reasons** – giving an opinion and listing reasons to accept that opinion. This type of organization makes it clear that the author wants to persuade the reader.

- **order of events** – telling about things in the order that they happened. A writer might use order of events to tell about a family vacation.

- **compare and contrast** – telling what is alike and different about two or more ideas. A writer might compare and contrast two TV shows to decide which is better.

You will learn more about how authors organize text in Lesson 9.

TIP 6: Compare one author's ideas to another's.

Don't take one author's word for it. Find out what someone else has to say. Look at more than one source of information on the topic. This is especially true if a writer is trying to persuade you to do or buy something.

Not everybody has the same opinion about everything. Some people like pepperoni on their pizza, but others would rather have green peppers. Two fans of the same baseball team may have different reasons for liking that team.

Two or more authors writing about the same topic may have different points of view. It can be helpful to notice how they agree and disagree. You should compare the opinions of different authors whenever you are assigned to write or speak about a topic.

Read the following paragraphs, then answer the questions that follow.

Author 1

Our school needs a new library. The present library is overflowing with too many books and bookshelves. Students have a hard time sitting comfortably to study. The big, new computer area has taken up a lot of space. Now that there are enough computers for everyone, we need a library that has plenty of space for books and students.

Author 2

Our school library needs to be replaced. It's much too crowded, especially when many students use it at the same time. Another problem is that the computer area is too small. It doesn't have enough computers for everyone. Books are nice, but we need fast computers to get along in the twenty-first century.

7. On which two ideas do the authors agree?

_____

_____

_____

8. What is one point about which the authors disagree?

_____

_____

_____

9. List some of the opinion words each author uses to persuade readers.

_____

_____

_____

 TIP 7: Think about other ways authors make their ideas clear.

An author's main job is to make readers understand his or her ideas. Without this skill, an author cannot persuade anybody. Authors have some tools to make sure their ideas are clear.

Sometimes authors explain important words. They give examples to support a point. Other times they may use a simple idea to describe a difficult one. For example, an author telling about stars might say this:

A star may look small in the sky, but it is a giant ball of gas like our sun.

Special type can help an author stress important information. An author may use *italics* to show that a word is used strongly. **Boldface** often shows that a word is important for understanding the topic. Authors may even use quotation marks to show that a word is being used in an unusual way.

Lesson Practice begins on the following page.

Directions: This passage tells about a woman who helped a sick friend. Read the passage. Then answer Numbers 1 through 8.

Signs of Life

by Mike Acton

Living in a Special Home

Mary Acton lives in a group home. It is a home for people who have a hard time living alone. She lives with friends who have become family to her. Mary and her friends take care of one another. All of the friends have special needs. They also share their home with a person who manages the house. In Mary's house, the manager is a woman named Pat. She looks out for the group and keeps the house in working order.

Life with Down Syndrome

Mary was born with Down syndrome. Down syndrome is a health problem that affects the body and mind. People with this condition have difficulty learning. Mary has lived with it all her life, but it hasn't stopped her from making great friends. She also does chores around the house.

When Mary isn't helping to clean, she likes to watch television with her friends. She loves to tell everyone what's on. That's why they call her "the TV Guide."

Mary's Time in School

Before she lived in the group home, Mary went to a school for special children. With the help of a caring teacher, Mary learned to use sign language. It is a way of making words with your hands. Using sign language is one of Mary's greatest talents. When she moved to the group home, she was able to "talk" to those who couldn't hear. Little did Mary know that her talent would soon save a life.

Mary Saves the Day

One night, Mary heard Pat making loud wheezing noises. Pat was suffering from an asthma attack. Asthma is an illness that affects a person's breathing. During an attack, someone like Pat can't breathe on her own. Luckily, Pat also knew sign language. Pat had just enough energy to "tell" Mary where her medicine was. Mary wasted no time. She quickly found the medicine and brought it to Pat. Mary saved Pat's life.

Because of her rescue, Mary was honored by many people. Some have called Mary Acton a hero. But she is still the quiet, caring person her friends have come to love. To Mary, it's not important to be a hero. It's enough to be a friend.

1. **What is the <u>most likely</u> reason the author wrote this passage?**

   A. to explain the importance of having friends

   B. to show readers that anyone can save a life

   C. to convince readers to learn sign language

   D. to give information about Down syndrome

2. **Read this sentence from the passage.**

   "Using sign language is one of Mary's greatest talents."

   Is this sentence a fact statement or an opinion? Why?

   _____

   _____

3. **Which detail from the passage supports the claim that Mary is a hero?**

   A. Mary lives with her friends.

   B. Mary learns sign language.

   C. Mary likes to watch television.

   D. Mary saves her friend's life.

4. **Which of these sentences contains an opinion word?**

   A. "With the help of a caring teacher, Mary learned to use sign language."

   B. "Asthma is an illness that affects a person's breathing."

   C. "They also share their home with a person who manages the house."

   D. "Down syndrome is a health problem that affects the body and mind."

5. **Read this sentence from the passage.**

    "Pat had just enough energy to 'tell' Mary where her medicine was."

    In this sentence, why does the author include quotation marks around *tell*?

    _____

    _____

6. **Why do Mary's roommates call her "the TV Guide"?**

    A. She is in charge of the television.

    B. She watches television instead of cleaning.

    C. She likes to tell others what's on television.

    D. She is the only one who can work the television.

7. **Which section of the passage explains what Down syndrome is?**

    _____

8. **What word from the passage means the same thing as *syndrome*?**

    A. condition

    B. chores

    C. needs

    D. manager

Lesson 9: Text Structures

Ideas can be arranged in many different ways. Understanding how ideas are arranged can make it easier to understand a passage. In this lesson, you'll learn about some of the most common ways in which authors put their ideas in order.

TIP 1: Some passages are arranged by the main idea and supporting details.

Remember, the main idea is what the passage is mainly about. Some authors usually begin with the main idea and list several details that describe or support it.

Read the following passage. Then answer Number 1.

Oil Lamps

A lamp is a device that makes light. There are three main kinds of lamps: oil lamps, gas lamps, and electric lamps.

An oil lamp, or fat lamp, burns grease, oil, or wax. Oil lamps were the first lamps, and they were made by prehistoric people. These people used seashells or hollowed-out rocks filled with animal fat. They made wicks, the stems that soak up the fatty oils and are lit, out of grass. Egyptians and Greeks made oil lamps that looked like a teakettle. The "kettle" part held the oil, and the spout held the wick, which was made from cotton. Later on, candles were invented. Candles are another kind of fat lamp.

Gas lamps have no wick. They produce light by burning gas near a small opening at the end of a gas tube. Gas lamps became very popular around 1800. They remained the best source of light until 1879.

In that year, Thomas Edison invented the first successful electric light. Electric lights became popular in the early 1900s. Today they have replaced other kinds of lamps for almost every use.

1. What is the main idea of the passage?

    A. A lamp is a device that makes light.

    B. There are three main kinds of lamps: oil lamps, gas lamps, and electric lamps.

    C. Oil lamps were the first lamps, and they were made by prehistoric people.

    D. Electric lights became popular in the early 1900s.

TIP 2: Some passages show how one event leads to another.

Some articles are written to show why something happened. This structure is called **cause and effect**. One event causes another event to happen. That second event is the effect. Then that effect causes another event to happen, and so on. When writing is arranged in this way, the author wants readers to understand how one thing causes others. Articles about events in history, science topics, and how-to texts are often structured this way.

Read the following passage. Then answer Number 2.

Mother of Invention

There is an old saying: "Necessity is the mother of invention." This saying means that when people really need something, they'll figure out a way to get it. In the case of Stephanie Kwolek, her needs led her to get a job. Then her company's needs led her to a great invention.

Kwolek dreamed of becoming a doctor, but she realized that she didn't have enough money to go to medical school. So, she had to get a job instead. Kwolek got a job working for a chemical company named DuPont.

For her job, she needed to find a way to make a light, strong material. Kwolek helped invent the material called Kevlar.

Kevlar is stronger than steel. Sometimes, police officers wear jackets made of Kevlar to help stop bullets. Some clothing for soldiers is made with Kevlar, too. Kevlar has also been used for things you see every day. In fact, it has even been used to make oven mitts.

Because Kevlar is a very important invention, Kwolek has been honored in the National Inventors Hall of Fame. She was the fourth woman to get into the Hall of Fame.

2. Fill in the boxes on the graphic organizer to show the cause-and-effect events in Stephanie Kwolek's life.

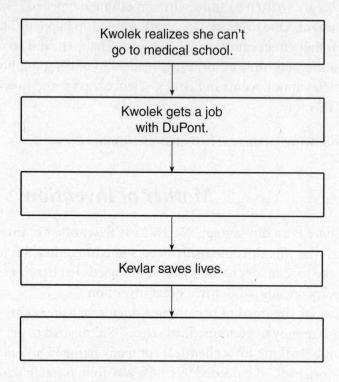

Kwolek realizes she can't
go to medical school.

Kwolek gets a job
with DuPont.

Kevlar saves lives.

 TIP 3: Look for cause words.

Certain words show when one thing causes another. This box shows some of the words that will help you spot causes and their effects.

Cause Words
cause
because
so
led to
due to
as a result of

CCSs: RI.4.3, RI.4.5

3. Read "Mother of Invention" again. Underline any words that help you find causes and effects.

 TIP 4: Connect the events in a *because* sentence.

If you don't see any cause words, put together details from the passage using the word *because*. For example, imagine that your friend Jeff says he is thirsty. Then Jeff drinks some water. You could write this sentence: "Jeff drank some water <u>because</u> he was thirsty." You can write a *because* sentence whenever you understand why something happened.

Read the following passage from an article about scallops. Scallops are a type of shellfish. The article is from *Ranger Rick* magazine. Pay attention to causes and effects.

> A scallop's gills are covered with thousands of tiny hairs called cilia that are too small to see. These hairs are always quickly waving back and forth. The waving sweeps water into the scallop's shell. The scallop gets oxygen from this water. And floating in the water are tiny plants and animals. They get caught on the cilia and are then swept into the scallop's mouth.

Now complete the following sentence based on what you have just read.

4. The cilia are helpful to the scallop because

_____

_____

Use your *because* sentence to answer the following question.

5. The movement of the cilia helps the scallop by

    A. keeping the scallop's gills warm in cold ocean waters.

    B. protecting the scallop from dangerous animals.

    C. bringing in water that contains oxygen and food.

    D. sweeping in water to clean the scallop's shell.

TIP 5: Some passages describe a problem and then give solutions.

Some authors tell readers about a problem first. Then they explain the steps that were taken to solve that problem.

Read the passage. Then answer the question that follows.

Ben Franklin's Stove

People who lived in early America suffered from cold winters. They needed to find a way to keep their houses warmer. People put fireplaces in their homes. The fireplaces were made of brick or stone and had chimneys for the smoke to escape. The fireplaces helped, but there were still problems. Fireplaces used a lot of wood, and although fires gave off heat, people were still cold in their homes.

A man from Philadelphia named Ben Franklin thought he could solve the problem. Franklin was a writer, printer, and scientist. He also was an inventor. Franklin thought he could make something better than a fireplace, but he had to figure out how to do it. He knew that iron was strong enough to hold fire. He decided to shape iron into a stove. The stove would be better than a fireplace, because it would provide more heat and make less smoke. Plus, the top of the stove could heat things like pots, pans, and kettles. Finally, he gave the invention to a friend who could build more of the iron stoves for other people. As more people learned about Franklin's invention, more people bought the iron stoves.

Today, people still use this invention. It is now known as the Franklin Stove.

6. Study this graphic organizer.

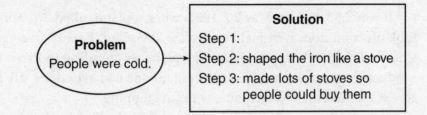

Which of the following best fills Step 1?

A. thought stoves would be a poor replacement for fireplaces

B. thought pots and pans could be set on a stove

C. decided that iron could safely contain fire

D. thought many stoves could be made and sold

Some authors begin by telling the reader about a problem. Then, the author will discuss some possible solutions for that problem.

Here's an example:

Problem: Your friend wants you to go to a movie, but you know there's going to be a surprise party for her that same day.

Solution 1: Tell your friend about the party.

Solution 2: Say you're not allowed to see any movies, ever.

Solution 3: Suggest that you and your friend see the movie on a different day.

TIP 6: Some passages describe events in the order in which they happened.

Some passages begin by telling what happened first, then next, and then last.

Read the following passage. Then answer Number 7.

Across the Atlantic

It was 7:52 A.M. on May 20, 1927, when a plane called *The Spirit of St. Louis* took off from Roosevelt Field near New York City. Twenty-five-year-old Charles Lindbergh was the pilot. The plane was heading to Paris, France. Lindbergh was trying to do something no one had ever done. He planned to fly across the Atlantic Ocean alone, without stopping.

First, he flew northeast along the coast of North America. Later in the afternoon he was spotted flying over Nova Scotia and Newfoundland. Then, Lindbergh turned out over the cold waters of the Atlantic as night fell. He was flying toward Ireland.

At 1:52 A.M. on May 21, Lindbergh was halfway to Paris. At 2:52 A.M., the sky began to lighten. It was dawn in the North Atlantic.

At 10:52 A.M., Lindbergh spotted the coast of Ireland. He had not expected to be at that point so early.

It was already evening in France. The sun set as he flew over the city of Cherbourg. About two and a half hours later, he landed in Paris. A cheering crowd was there to greet him when he touched down at 10:22 P.M. He had flown for 33 and a half hours straight.

7. Study this graphic organizer.

Lindbergh's Solo Flight

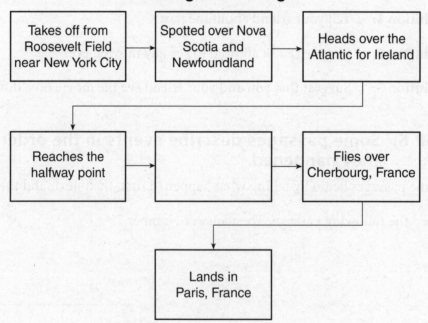

According to the passage, which of the following belongs in the empty box?

A. Night falls

B. Sees Ireland

C. Takes a short nap

D. Greeted by cheering crowd

TIP 7: Some passages are organized to show how things are alike or different.

To **compare** two things is to show how they are alike. To **contrast** things is to show how they are different. The following passage shows things that are alike and different in the ways a boy and his dog walk home after school during the week. It is from *Henry Huggins* by Beverly Cleary.

Every afternoon after school, Ribsy waited for Henry under a fir tree in the corner of the school yard. Four days a week they ran home the shortest way, past the park, up the hill, and through the vacant lot. On Fridays, however, they walked home the long way, round past the Rose City Drugstore, the Supermarket, the Ideal Barber Shop, and the Lucky Dog Pet Shop.

8. What is different about the way Henry and Ribsy walk home on Fridays?

A. They take a longer path.

B. They meet under a fir tree.

C. They go past the park.

D. They go through a vacant lot.

Lesson Practice begins on the following page.

Directions: This passage tells about the person who created a children's baseball program. Read the passage. Then answer Numbers 1 through 8.

Real Uniforms, Real Ballparks

by Tom Fitzpatrick

In 1939, Carl Stotz had an exciting idea. His two nephews loved baseball. Until then, kids could only play in backyards and in the street. Stotz, who also loved baseball, wanted his nephews to be part of a real team. He wanted them to have real uniforms to wear and a real ballpark to play in. So, Stotz got the idea to start an organized league for children who liked to play baseball. After a lot of searching, he found three businesses that were willing to help. They gave Stotz money to get started. With that, Little League Baseball was born.

Over the next few years, more teams formed in other towns. In 1947, the first Little League World Series was held. Before long, teams had formed all over the country. But Little League didn't stop at the U.S. borders. People began to form teams in other countries.

Soon there were teams in Panama, Cuba, Canada, and Puerto Rico. In 1957, a Mexican team won the Little League World Series. It was the first team from outside the U.S. to win. Angel Macias was the team's star player. When he returned to Mexico, he was treated as a hero. Baseball had truly become a world sport.

Little League's fame kept spreading. In 1963, the Little League World Series was shown on national television. By then, a new ballpark had been built for the event.

More and more kids wanted to play Little League. So, Little League started other kinds of teams. Farm teams were created to train younger players. Junior and Senior Leagues were organized for older players. In 1974, Little League started a girls' softball league. Little League became the largest youth-sports group in the country.

Little League teaches important character skills such as loyalty and teamwork. These skills are useful in school, work, and play. Hundreds of Little Leaguers have even gone on to play Major League Baseball.

Americans have played baseball for years. Now kids from around the world take part in Little League each year. And they get to wear real uniforms when they do.

1. **This passage is <u>mostly</u> organized by**

    A. cause and effect.

    B. problem and solution.

    C. main idea and supporting details.

    D. order of events.

2. **Why did Carl Stotz start Little League Baseball?**

    _____

    _____

    _____

    _____

3. **Which of the following statements from the passage is an opinion?**

    A. "Little League became the largest youth-sports group in the country."

    B. "In 1947, the first Little League World Series was held."

    C. "But Little League didn't stop at the U.S. borders."

    D. "Little League teaches important character skills such as loyalty and teamwork."

4. **What is the author's purpose for writing this passage?**

   _____

   _____

   _____

5. **What is the main idea of the passage?**

   A. Children play Little League Baseball around the world.

   B. Little League grew from a small club to a worldwide group.

   C. Real uniforms and ballparks make baseball more fun to play.

   D. All Major League Baseball players began by playing Little League.

6. **What problem did Carl Stotz solve by starting Little League Baseball?**

   _____

   _____

   _____

7. **Which of the following statements from the passage is a fact?**

    A. "In 1939, Carl Stotz had an exciting idea."

    B. "Soon there were teams in Panama, Cuba, Canada, and Puerto Rico."

    C. "Baseball had truly become a world sport."

    D. "These skills are useful in school, work, and play."

8. **According to the passage, how does Little League help young ballplayers?**

    _____

    _____

    _____

    _____

Lesson 10: Information You Can See

Most of the time, you have to read in order to get information. But some kinds of information are easier to understand when you can see them. In this lesson, you will practice getting information from pictures, tables, and other sources you can see.

TIP 1: A diagram names the parts of the subject.

Some articles come with special pictures called diagrams. A **diagram** shows a picture of something the article talks about, with all of its parts named. The parts may be pieces of a computer, muscles in a person's leg, or the steps in a dance. Diagrams appear in articles, textbooks, and other nonfiction texts. Often you will see diagrams included in a set of instructions for putting something together. The diagrams will show you the steps for putting that thing together.

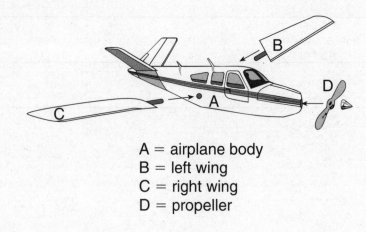

A = airplane body
B = left wing
C = right wing
D = propeller

1. Based on the model airplane diagram, which part is the propeller attached to?

    A. airplane body

    B. left wing

    C. right wing

    D. tail

TIP 2: Use a map to help you understand places.

Some articles will include maps to help you understand the location of places in an area. For example, an article about a new U.S. highway in a specific area might give you a map of the area.

Look at the following example.

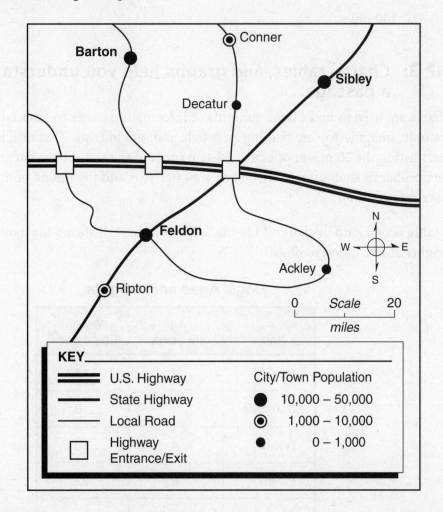

Most maps have a **key** that tells what the symbols on the map mean. The **compass** shows how the map relates to the four directions: north, south, east, and west. And the **scale** shows how many miles are represented by a unit of measure on the map. On this map, one inch equals 20 miles.

123

Carefully look at the map, key, and the scale. Then answer Number 2.

2. The distance between Decatur and Conner is approximately

   A. 2 miles.

   B. 10 miles.

   C. 50 miles.

   D. 100 miles.

TIP 3: Charts, tables, and graphs help you understand a passage.

Charts are used to make large amounts of information easier to understand. For example, imagine you are reading an article about field trips. That article might have a chart listing the 20 most popular field-trip spots in the state. The chart might also show the number of students who visit each spot per year and the phone numbers to call for more information.

A **table** is one kind of chart. Study the following chart. It shows the names, ages, and weights of five different dogs.

Dogs' Ages and Weights

Name	Age (in years)	Weight (in pounds)
Max	2	14
Sunshine	1	8
Rocky	4	38
Flash	9	22
Lady	3	6

3. Which dog weighs the most?

_____

4. How old is the dog that weighs 14 pounds?

_____

CCS: RI.4.7

Bar graphs and pie charts are two other kinds of charts. **Bar graphs** compare different amounts of the same kinds of thing. **Pie charts** show how parts of a whole compare with each other. Look at the following bar graph and pie chart. They show the same information about the favorite pizza toppings chosen by 21 students.

Study the bar graph. Find how many students chose each topping.

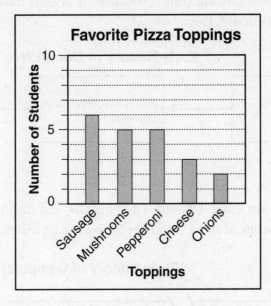

Now study the pie chart. Notice how it shows the students' choices as an entire group.

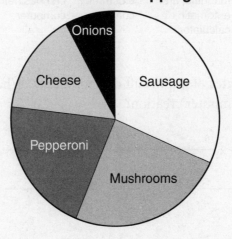

5. Which topping was the favorite of the most students?

_____

TIP 4: Timelines help you see the order of events.

A **timeline** is a picture that shows the order of events. For example, it can show events from history or steps in a science project. A timeline can also help you map out what order important details were given in a text.

Take a look at the following simple timeline. It doesn't have dates or times on it, but it does show events in order.

Early History of Computers

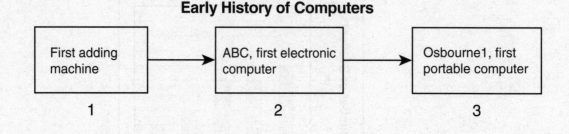

Other timelines are more detailed. They may list important dates in history or show a more complex series of steps. Read the following timeline, and answer Number 6.

Early History of Computers

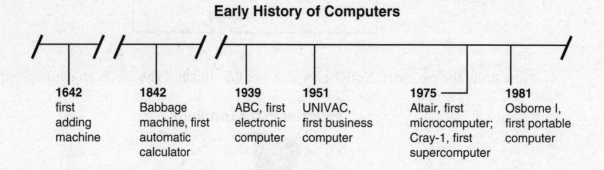

6. Look at the dates of important developments. What can you tell about the speed of changes in computer creation?

_____

_____

CCS: RI.4.7

TIP 5: Interactive elements can help you understand what you read on a computer.

Reading on a computer can be very different from reading a book. Web sites use more than words and pictures. They can also include videos and sounds. **Interactive elements** are features the reader can control. For example, you can pause a video or watch it again.

Some sounds may include music, sound effects, or speech. An **oral presentation** is a speech about a topic. You may be able to listen to someone reading the text of the page aloud.

Other features allow readers to add to the site. You can often write a note about what you have read. You might get to add your own picture or video. A **webcam** is a camera that sends images to a Web site.

You might get to play a video game. Some games can help you understand what you read. Imagine you are reading an article about ant farms. It might include a short game in which you build your own farm.

Another common feature is the hyperlink, or link for short. **Links** are highlighted words that you can click on with the mouse. Clicking on a link changes what you see on the screen. It may show a different section of what you are reading. Or it may take you to another Web site.

TIP 6: Animations are pictures in motion.

Some Web sites include a feature called an animation. An **animation** is a picture that moves. It looks like a cartoon. It may use simple motion to show how something works. You can more easily understand how a bicycle works if you see it moving.

7. How is an animation like a diagram?

   A. It looks like a cartoon.

   B. It uses simple motions.

   C. It shows how things work.

   D. It labels the parts of things.

Lesson Practice begins on the following page.

Directions: This passage is about finding gold in the Black Hills. Read the passage. Then answer Numbers 1 through 8.

Hills of Gold

by Rick Zollo

It all began in 1876, when Moses and Fred Manuel discovered a vein of gold ore. It was called a "lead" because it would lead miners to larger deposits. The lead was found just outside the town of Deadwood in the Black Hills of South Dakota. At the time, the Black Hills were swarming with men searching for gold. The Manuel brothers had found what would turn out to be the area's richest strike.

The Black Hills

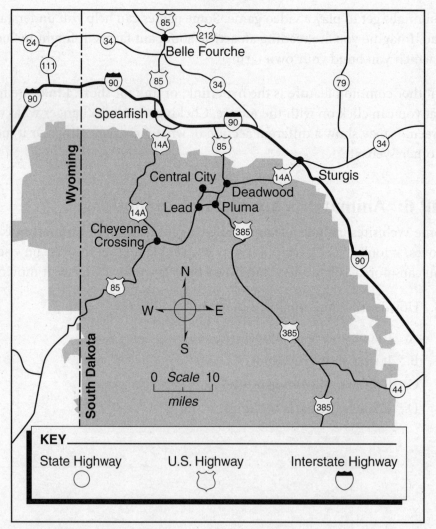

Homestake Mining Company

In the following year, the Manuels formed the Homestake Mining Company. They helped found a booming new mining town called Lead. Three years later, the first railroad entered the Black Hills. The railroad helped to bring in supplies and to ship out the gold. The Homestake claim eventually grew into two different mines. One was a large and ever-growing open pit. This mine was for reaching gold that was close to the surface. Today this hole is more than 800 feet deep. (Figure 1 shows what an open-pit mine looks like.) The other was a much richer underground mine that went down more than 8,000 feet into the earth. That is one and a half miles deep. (Figure 2 shows what an underground mine looks like.)

By 1900, the mine was producing more than 170,000 ounces of gold a year. By 1910, that figure rose to 225,000. Miners kept improving their methods. By 1935, more than half a million ounces had been taken from the Homestake. For decades after, the mine kept producing those kinds of numbers.

Figure 1 – Open-Pit Gold Mine

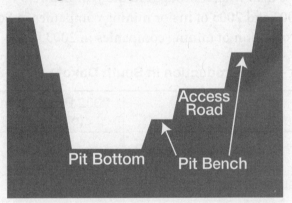

Figure 2 – Underground Gold Mine

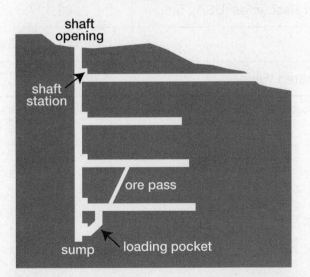

Closing the Mine

The Black Hills of South Dakota have many wonders, none richer than the Homestake Gold Mine. It was the longest continuously operating gold mine in the world until it shut down. Although there is still plenty of gold in the mine, the Homestake claim has stopped production.

By the 1990s, the price of gold had dropped so low that many gold mines had to close. It was just too costly to get the ore out of the ground. In 2000, after having produced a whopping 40 million ounces (1,250 tons) of gold since its opening, the company decided not to keep the mine running. The open-pit mine had produced all the gold that was worth mining above ground. And the Homestake underground mine could no longer overcome low gold prices, high mining costs, and the lower-quality gold coming from the mine. In January 2002, the mine closed down. During the destruction of its mill, a final 7,754 ounces of gold was produced.

Despite the drop in the price of gold, the mineral continues to be a valuable product for South Dakota. In 2003, gold production brought in $28.6 million, and that was 22 percent less than what it brought in the year before. Figure 3 compares gold production for 2002 and 2003 of major mining companies in South Dakota. Figure 4 compares gold production of mining companies in 2003.

Figure 3 – Gold Production in South Dakota 2002–2003

Company	2002 Production (ounces)	2003 Production (ounces)
Golden Reward Mining Co., LP	50	0
Homestake Mining Company	36,334	7,754
LAC Minerals (USA), LLC	0	149
Wharf Resources (USA), Inc.	82,127	70,902
Total	118,511	78,805
Estimated Value	$36,706,412	$28,636,161

Source: South Dakota Department of Environment and Natural Resources

Figure 4 – Gold Production in South Dakota 2003

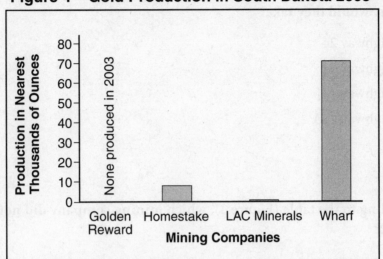

Source: South Dakota Department of Environment and Natural Resources

The Future of Homestake

Luckily for Lead and the Black Hills, Homestake is repairing all the areas it disturbed with its huge open-pit mine. The project is expected to take eight years and cost about $66 million.

Currently, both mines sit in the heart of the Black Hills as tourist attractions. Visitors can travel into the open pit or visit the underground mine museum.

At one time in our history, people braved great danger to head into the wilderness, finding gold in such places as the hills of South Dakota and California, and in the frozen north of Alaska. Gold fueled the dreams of many adventurous men and women. Today, visitors can see the remains of those dreams at the Homestake Claim.

1. Based on the map, if travelers wanted to go from Deadwood to Sturgis, which highway would they take?

    A. Highway 24

    B. Highway 34

    C. Highway 111

    D. Highway 14A

2. According to the table (Figure 3), which mining company did <u>not</u> produce any gold in 2002?

    _____

3. How does the bar graph (Figure 4) help you understand the mines' production in a way that the table (Figure 3) does not?

    _____

    _____

4. If this passage appeared on a Web site, which feature would <u>most likely</u> help to show how mining works?

    A. animation

    B. hyperlink

    C. video game

    D. webcam

5. Which section of the passage gives information about Homestake ending production?

    _____

6. What is the <u>main</u> way the author organizes this passage?

    A. order of events

    B. cause and effect

    C. problem and solution

    D. compare and contrast

7. Why was Homestake Mine shut down? Use two details from the passage to support your answer.

    _____

    _____

    _____

8. Why did the author include the diagrams of the open-pit mine (Figure 1) and underground mine (Figure 2)? What differences do the diagrams show?

    _____

    _____

    _____

    _____

Lesson 11: Comparing Passages

Authors can deal with the same subject in many different ways. Every author makes choices about what to include, what to leave out, and what to make most important. You can learn new things about a story or event if you read what different people wrote about it.

Comparing Nonfiction Passages

When you go to a library to find information, you will probably find many books and articles written about the subject in which you are interested. The following tips will help you figure out what is alike and different in texts about the same subject. They will also show you how to put all of the information together.

Read the following two accounts of the same event. Look carefully to see how they are alike and different.

Here is an eyewitness account from a passenger's diary, in which she describes the sinking of the ship *Titanic* in 1912.

> Mother told me not to look, but I just had to: the world's largest luxury liner was sinking into the sea. Mother put both hands over my ears, but I could still hear the cries from those we left behind.
>
> The waters were freezing cold and full of ice chunks. No one could survive for long in these waters. Most of the people in our lifeboat were women, children, and [weak] old men. We shivered in the cold, damp air. I couldn't help but think of the hundreds of people who had stayed aboard and gone down with the ship.
>
> We drifted on a smooth sea for hours, with several other lifeboats around us. Where were our rescuers? The great, unsinkable *Titanic* was no more, and we, its survivors, wondered if we would ever be found.
>
> Just as the sky began to lighten in the east, a woman pointed and gave a cheer. After freezing for six hours in an open boat, a great ship was approaching to rescue us. Later, we learned that the ship was called the *Carpathia*.

CCSs: RI.4.6, RI.4.10

The second account comes from a news story in the *New York Times*, April 16, 1912.

CAPE RACE, Newfoundland, April 16—The White Star liner *Olympic* reports by its [radio] this evening that the . . . *Carpathia* reached, at daybreak this morning, the position from which wireless calls for help were sent out last night by the *Titanic* after her collision with an iceberg. The *Carpathia* found only the lifeboats and the wreckage of what had been the biggest steamship afloat.

The *Titanic* had [gone down] at about 2:20 A.M. . . . All her boats are accounted for and about 655 lives have been saved of the crew and passengers, most of [whom were] women and children.

TIP 1: Determine how the topics of the two passages work together.

When you're asked to compare passages, first see how each passage deals with its topic. In this case, both passages tell about different people and different events, but both touch on the same general topic. Also, each passage was written from a different point of view and for a different purpose.

1. Which of the following best describes the topic of both passages?

   A. riding in a lifeboat

   B. the crew of the *Carpathia*

   C. the sinking of the *Titanic*

   D. how steamships work

TIP 2: Compare main ideas and details between the passages.

To **compare** things is to show how they are alike and different. When comparing passages about the same topic, think about the main ideas and details of each piece of writing. How are they alike and different? What details about the setting or events does one author include that the other author doesn't? Also know that you can compare main ideas and details when reading fictional passages, too.

2. What is the main idea of the diary entry?

_____

_____

135

3. What is the main idea of the newspaper article?

_____

_____

 TIP 3: Compare the purpose of each passage.

Keep in mind the purpose of each passage you read and what kind of writing the author is doing. Is the passage written as current news? Is the passage written years after the event? Is the passage written to inform, to entertain, or to persuade? Writers usually have a goal in mind when they write.

4. What is the purpose of the diary entry?

_____

_____

5. What is the purpose of the newspaper article?

_____

_____

 TIP 4: Compare firsthand and secondhand accounts of events.

Firsthand accounts are written by people who saw what happened. **Secondhand** accounts are written by people who were not there. The writers have learned what they can in order to write about it.

When reading two texts about the same event, notice how the accounts are different. A secondhand writer may be able to gather more information about an event. A firsthand writer may be better able to explain how it felt. Sometimes the people, places, and events in one passage will help you better understand another.

Think about the two passages you just read. Then answer Number 6.

6. Which of the two passages was a firsthand account?

_____

CCSs: RL.4.9, RI.4.9

TIP 5: Use information from multiple passages when reporting on a topic.

Often you won't find all you need to know about a topic from reading just one passage. You'll need to read a few articles by different authors. As you read, take notes about the important details of each. Then, put your notes together. Using details from multiple passages in a speech or report will make you look like an expert on your topic.

7. What information is found in the diary entry but not in the news article?

_____

_____

8. What information is found in both passages?

_____

_____

Comparing Fictional Passages

There are thousands upon thousands of stories on Earth. Some are new stories and others are very, very old. Are all of these stories about different things? No. Many different authors write stories about the same things. The following are more tips to show you how to compare and contrast stories.

TIP 6: Compare stories from around the world to learn how people share the same feelings.

Stories from different countries often share themes. A **theme** is a lesson that a story teaches. It is not only true for the people in the story but for life in general. When we compare themes, we see that people everywhere are alike.

Certain themes are very common. For example, many stories concern the struggle between good and evil. There are certain types of stories that are told around the world, as well. Many stories tell of heroes on a quest, which is a long search for something important.

Myths and traditional stories have been told for many years in different ways. **Myths** are tales of gods and heroes. They often explain natural events. Stories from every part of the world tell how Earth was created.

Traditional stories are passed down from parents to children over hundreds of years. They include fairy tales and folktales like "Little Red Riding Hood." Many were made up before people knew how to write. Because they were not written down, they changed over the years. As the stories traveled between countries, storytellers changed the details. But the basic ideas stayed the same. They include lessons about working hard, staying safe, and being kind to others.

Some traditional stories include "Cinderella," "Sleeping Beauty," "Snow White," and "Hansel and Gretel." You could hear one of these stories in Kenya, India, or Iceland. The names and events may be different. But each telling touches on the same truths about life.

TIP 7: Use one passage to help you understand another.

Sometimes the setting, characters, and actions in one passage will help you better understand the characters and actions in another. Making connections between passages will also help you better understand the overall theme.

TIP 8: Think about who is telling each story.

When reading stories, it's important to know who is telling each story. If any two people tell the same story, both will tell it differently. What is important to one storyteller may not be important to another.

Notice who is narrating each story. Is the story told from the first-person point of view or third-person point of view? Remember that a first-person narrator is a character in the story. A third-person narrator is outside the story. A first-person narrator knows only what the character knows. A third-person narrator knows what every character knows.

First-person narrators also put their own twist on stories. Their feelings affect how they tell about the setting, events, and even the other characters.

Imagine a story about a girl moving to a new town. The girl is scared of her new neighbor's dog. If the girl tells the story, she will describe the dog in a scary way. An outside narrator may show that the dog is loud but friendly.

TIP 9: You can compare fiction and nonfiction passages with one another.

You can compare a fiction passage with a nonfiction passage. For example, you could compare a made-up story and a true story about someone's life. Sometimes two passages can seem very different. But once you look at the parts more closely, you'll see that the passages are more alike than you thought!

Lesson Practice begins on the following page.

Directions: These passages both tell about Goldilocks meeting the three bears. Read each passage. Then answer Numbers 1 through 8.

Goldilocks's Story

I couldn't believe I got lost. I had left home for a short walk, and suddenly I didn't know where I was. I shouldn't have wandered so far. I decided to knock on the door of a nice little house I spotted through the trees. No one answered, so I knocked a little louder. I guessed no one was home.

I was quite tired and terribly hungry, and I couldn't see another house for miles. I was starting to worry that I might not get home by nightfall. I decided to try the door. It had been left unlocked. Normally I wouldn't have done something like this, but I went inside. I was sure the owners would have felt sorry for me and let me in, if they had been home.

It looked like whoever lived there just got up and left in the middle of breakfast. That was lucky for me! I had three different bowls of porridge to choose from. I noticed something strange, though. Why were they all different temperatures? The first two I tried were not good. But the last one was perfect. Yum! I wondered if it was rude to lick the bowl if no one could see you. Finally, my stomach stopped grumbling.

I couldn't leave yet. My legs were still tired from walking around, trying to find my way back home. I needed to sit down, just for a little while. I hoped the people who lived there wouldn't mind. There were some cozy-looking chairs in the kitchen. One of them seemed like a perfect fit for someone my size. But as I sat down—whoops! It must have been made for someone smaller than I am! Now the chair was just a pile of sticks.

I thought maybe I should just find a place to lie down. A tummy full of warm porridge had made me sleepy. A little nap would do me good before I tried to find my way back home. I started to look around upstairs. There were beds up there. I lay down in one and let out a yelp. "Ouch!" This bed was way too hard. It hurt! So I tried another one, but it wasn't right at all. It was way too soft.

I wondered if there was another bed in the room down the hall. There was, and it was perfect! I fit on it nicely, and it wasn't too hard or too soft. I just closed my eyes for a short nap.

Father Bear's Story

What a morning it was! It all began when Mother Bear gave Little Bear his breakfast. I knew he was tired of eating porridge for breakfast every morning. In fact, I was tired of porridge, too. But Little Bear shouldn't have run out of the house and into the woods because he didn't want his porridge. The woods were no place for Little Bear to roam alone. So Mother Bear and I dropped our spoons and took off into the woods after him.

We finally found Little Bear wandering by the stream, and Mother Bear and I persuaded him to come back home. I told him that I understood he was tired of porridge, but until he was old enough to make his own breakfast, he would have to eat what Mother Bear made. Now we had to get back home to finish our breakfast. My porridge would certainly be cold.

Soon we were home. As I opened the door, something made me stop. Little Bear's bowl of porridge was empty now. How could this be? He was happy that someone had eaten it for him. But who could have gobbled the porridge down?

And what did I see next? It looked like a pile of firewood where Little Bear's kitchen chair used to be. What was going on here? Had someone broken into our house while we were out? Why would someone break a chair? I began to fear what else we might find, or who might have been here.

Mother Bear, Little Bear, and I walked around the rest of the house to make sure nothing else was touched. I decided to check upstairs. My room was fine, but I thought I had made the bed before breakfast. Mother Bear's room was fine, but the sheets on her bed were messed up, too.

Next, I checked Little Bear's room. I was in for a shock. There was a little girl with long, golden locks sleeping in Little Bear's bed. She was the one! This crook had broken into our house. This thief had stolen our food. This monster had broken our chair! And now she had the nerve to sleep in my child's bed! I was so angry, I didn't know what to do.

Then I knew. I would wake her up with my loudest growl and scare her off. That would teach her not to make trouble with bears.

1. **Which of the following details appears in both passages?**

    A.   Goldilocks licks clean Little Bear's bowl.

    B.   Father Bear is angry.

    C.   Goldilocks is sleeping in Little Bear's bed.

    D.   Little Bear runs away.

2. **What point of view is "Goldilocks's Story" told from?**

    _____

3. **Which of the following details is only found in "Goldilocks's Story"?**

    A.   Little Bear doesn't eat his porridge.

    B.   Little Bear's chair is a pile of broken wood.

    C.   Goldilocks needs to rest her legs.

    D.   Father Bear notices Little Bear's bowl is empty.

4. **How does "Goldilocks's Story" help you to understand "Father Bear's Story"?**

    _____

    _____

    _____

5. **What is the author's purpose for writing "Father Bear's Story"?**

   A. to explain why Goldilocks ate the porridge

   B. to let the reader know how Father Bear feels

   C. to show how Goldilocks feels about the bears

   D. to teach readers not to wander far from home

6. **Father Bear is angry about what Goldilocks has done. How is this different from what Goldilocks expects?**

   _____

   _____

   _____

7. **What is the main problem in "Father Bear's Story"?**

   A. Little Bear will not eat his porridge.

   B. Someone has broken into the bears' home.

   C. Father Bear's porridge has gotten cold.

   D. Mother Bear cooks too much porridge.

8. **How does Father Bear solve this problem?**

   _____

   _____

   _____

UNIT 2

Writing

Writing can seem like a scary task. This unit will help you break the writing process into small steps. First, you'll learn to think about who will read your writing. Then, you will learn how to plan your writing using a graphic organizer. Next, you'll write a draft of your essay or story. Then, you will learn how to edit, revise, and proofread your writing, brushing up on your grammar skills along the way. Finally, you will explore ways to publish your final draft. It is likely that your teacher will ask you to write an essay using a specific writing form. You may even be asked to do this on a writing test. Later in the unit you will learn about some different forms of writing. The lessons will give you useful tips on how to write in these forms.

If you take the time to organize and polish your ideas, you will end up with a piece of writing you can be proud of.

In This Unit

Planning

Drafting

Revising, Editing, and Publishing

Writing Opinions

Writing to Inform

Narrative Writing

Research and Information

Writing a Response

Lesson 12: Planning

If you wanted to jump as far and as high as you could, how would you do it? Would you stand still and just jump? Or would you warm up a little, think about what you were going to do, and then take a running start?

If you want to write as well as you can, you usually need to warm up a little, too. Prewriting is a way to give yourself a running start before you write an essay, a story, or any other type of writing.

Before you can write, you need something to write about. You also need to put your ideas in order so they make sense.

Prewriting is the planning you do before you write. Prewriting activities can help you get ideas for a topic or figure out what to say about a topic. In addition, prewriting can help you make sense of the ideas you have about a topic.

TIP 1: Understand your purpose, audience, topic, and form.

There are four things to consider when you begin planning to write.

- What is your **purpose**? Ask yourself, "Why am I writing? What do I hope readers will think?"

- Who is your **audience**? Think about who will read your writing. How should you write for this audience?

- What is your **topic**? Think about the subject you are going to write about. Ask yourself, "What do I know about it? What do I need to find out?"

- What is the **form** of your writing? Think about how you will present your writing. Will you write an essay, a story, or something else?

Your teacher or another adult can often help you answer these questions. Other students can also give you ideas about what you should write about.

Imagine that your teacher wants you to write about an animal from the Amazon Rain Forest. This is what she tells you:

> This week we will be studying the Amazon Rain Forest. You will choose an animal from that area to write about. Find out all that you can about where the animal lives, what it eats, and any other interesting facts. Your classmates will read your description of this animal. You should give your classmates as much information as you can about the animal you choose.

Before you begin writing, your teacher asks you to answer questions about the purpose, audience, topic, and form for the assignment. Here are the questions you asked and your answers:

Purpose: Why am I writing?

to give information

Audience: Who will read my writing?

my classmates

Topic: What am I writing about?

an animal from the Amazon Rain Forest

Form: What kind of writing am I doing (an informational report, a story response, and so on)?

an informational report

Anytime you are given a writing topic, answer these four questions first.

Read the assignment below. Then answer Numbers 1 through 4.

> The Happy Thoughts Greeting Card Company is holding an essay contest. The winner will be allowed to create a new national holiday. People entering the contest are asked to describe the holiday they would like to create. What would the holiday celebrate? On what day should it be held? How would people celebrate this new holiday? Think about the holiday you would like to create. Start planning your essay to enter the contest.

1. **Purpose:** Why am I writing?

   _____

2. **Audience:** For whom am I writing?

   _____

3. **Topic:** What am I writing about?

_____

4. **Form:** What kind of writing am I doing (a persuasive letter, a true story, a descriptive essay, and so on)?

_____

 ## TIP 2: Brainstorm ideas.

A topic will usually be assigned to you. But how do you come up with ideas about your topic? Brainstorm. **Brainstorming** is simple: Just grab a pencil and a piece of paper and start writing anything that pops into your mind about your topic. Write as fast as you can. Even if the ideas seem a little mixed up or silly, write them down. You can even pair up with a classmate or work in a group to brainstorm ideas together.

Later, you can decide which ideas you want to keep. You can throw the rest away or save them for another writing project. First, just try to come up with as many ideas as you can—as fast as you can. Write all over the page. Underline things. Make idea webs. Draw circles around important words.

Brainstorming, as the word says, creates a storm of lightning flashes in your mind. Ideas thunder in your head. Thoughts fall onto your paper like raindrops. One student's brainstorm for the essay about a new national holiday looks like this:

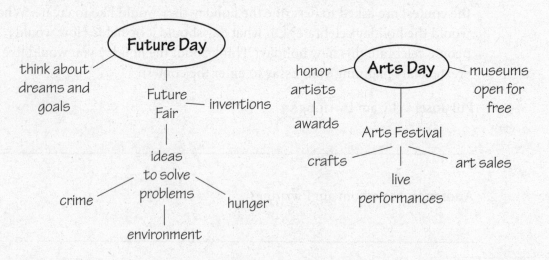

TIP 3: Another fast way to gather ideas is called freewriting.

To **freewrite**, simply write about your topic in paragraph form as fast as you can, without stopping. Don't worry about capitalization, punctuation, grammar, or spelling. (You can work on these things later.) Just get your thoughts down on paper.

Freewriting takes only a few minutes (two or three minutes is usually long enough) and can produce dozens of ideas about a topic. Here is an example:

> An arts day would be fun for towns to celebrate. An arts festival could be held where artists would do live performances like dancing, music, plays, painting. artists could sell their stuff and help people make their own crafts and things. All ages. Awards could be given to the best artists i think artists would like some money as a prize. Museums could open for free for the day, What else to say? What to say? this holiday should be held on a weekend day in the summer so that many people can enjoy it.

This paragraph is far from being finished, but the writer is off to a pretty good start.

Putting Ideas in Order

After you gather your ideas, you must organize them. To **organize** is to put your ideas in an order that makes sense. There are many different ways to organize ideas. But there is one order that should guide everything you write.

TIP 4: Your writing needs a beginning, middle, and an end.

A train needs an engine, cars, and a caboose. In the same way, your writing needs a beginning, a middle, and an end. When you write an essay, your "train of thought" might look like this:

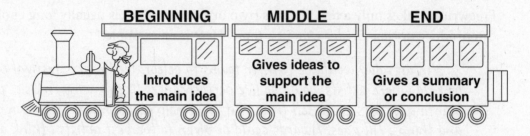

BEGINNING — Introduces the main idea

MIDDLE — Gives ideas to support the main idea

END — Gives a summary or conclusion

For example, imagine that you are asked to write about something that could be done to care for Earth. You decide to write about recycling. Here is one way you might organize your information.

Recycle to Save the Earth

Beginning	
• Introduce my topic. • Tell why my topic is interesting.	Tell what recycling is. Tell that recycling can help with many problems in the world.
Middle	
• Give ideas to support my topic. • Give details about the ideas.	**Idea:** Tell about how recycling helps with the problems of too much trash. Detail: Recycling lessens need for landfills, which can make water and air dirty. **Idea:** Tell about how recycling helps save resources. Detail: Recycling paper saves thousands of trees each year.
End	
• Briefly summarize my topic and the most important points.	Tell why it is a good idea to recycle.

CCSs: W.4.4, W.4.5

5. Nate is writing about different ways he has traveled. Below are the ideas he has for his writing. Help him organize his information by drawing a line connecting each idea to the part of the train it should go with.

Nate's Travels

Tell about experience with airplane travel.

I have taken many trips, traveling lots of different ways.

Tell about experience with train travel.

Tell about experience with car travel.

Tell about experience with ship travel.

Traveling by airplane, train, car, and ship are all very different ways to get to where you're going.

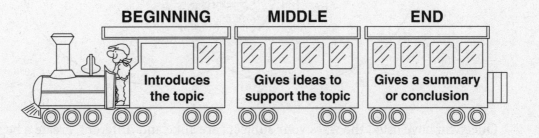

BEGINNING — Introduces the topic

MIDDLE — Gives ideas to support the topic

END — Gives a summary or conclusion

Once you know how your ideas should be put together, it is helpful to make a beginning-middle-end chart. You can make one like the one on page 148. When you begin writing your draft, you can look at your chart. You'll know just what to write about.

TIP 5: **If you plan to compare two things, use a Venn diagram to organize your ideas.**

In some of your writing, you may want to compare and contrast two things. To **compare and contrast** means to show how things are alike and different. Before you begin writing, make a list of facts about each subject you are comparing. You can list the ways they are alike and different using a Venn diagram.

A **Venn diagram** is a picture that shows how things are alike and different. Ideas about one subject appear in one circle. Ideas about another subject appear in another circle. Where the circles cross, the ideas describe both subjects.

For example, imagine that you are asked to compare a train and a bus. Here is one way you might organize your information.

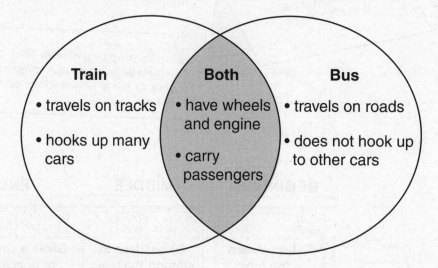

Once you have listed the ways your subjects are alike and different, create a beginning-middle-end chart to plan your writing.

CCSs: W.4.4, W.4.5

6. Use the Venn diagram that follows to list ways in which a dog and a frog are alike and different.

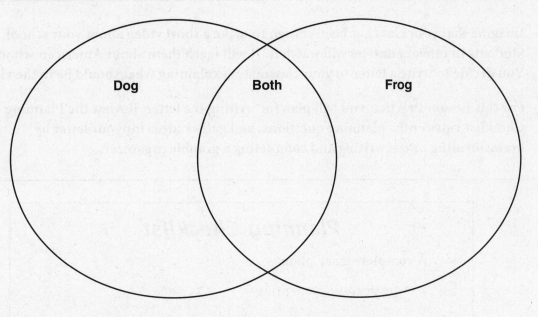

Dog   Both   Frog

 TIP 6: You can organize your writing in other ways.

Explaining how things are alike and different is not the only way to organize your writing. Three more ways to organize your writing are listed here.

*   **sequence (order of events):** When you write about events in sequence, you write about them in the order that they happen. If you are telling the main events in a story, you would most likely begin with the events that happened first and work your way up to what happened last.

*   **cause and effect:** When you use cause and effect to organize your writing, you are showing the reader how one thing leads to another.

*   **problem and solution:** When you organize your writing around a problem and solution, first you state the problem and then you find ways to solve the problem. The end of your essay should provide a clear solution to the problem.

Lesson Practice begins on the following page.

Planning

Imagine that your class has been chosen to make a short video about your school. Students in other countries will watch it. It will teach them about American schools. You decide to write a letter to your classmates explaining what should be in the video.

For this Lesson Practice, you will plan for writing the letter. Review the Planning Checklist, answer the planning questions, and gather ideas for your letter by brainstorming or freewriting and completing a graphic organizer.

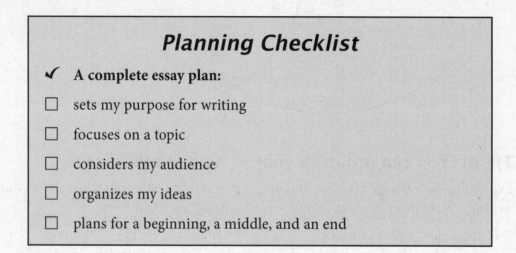

Planning Checklist

✓ **A complete essay plan:**

☐ sets my purpose for writing

☐ focuses on a topic

☐ considers my audience

☐ organizes my ideas

☐ plans for a beginning, a middle, and an end

Directions: Answer the following questions about your topic.

1. Why am I writing?

   _____

   _____

2. Who am I writing for?

   _____

   _____

3. What am I writing about?

   _____

   _____

4. What kind of writing am I doing?

   _____

   _____

Directions: Freewrite or brainstorm in the space below.

Directions: Fill in the beginning-middle-end chart with information about your topic.

Beginning:	
Middle:	
End:	

CCS: W.4.4

Lesson 13: Drafting

Have you ever had a conversation like this?

> Lindsey: Hey, Aaron. Wanna hear about a scary movie I saw on Saturday?
>
> Aaron: Sure. I went to a ball game with Dale that day.
>
> Lindsey: Really? I heard that Dale got a new puppy.
>
> Aaron: Yeah. And Jan just got a pet parrot, like the ones in the zoo.
>
> Lindsey: Cool! I like the birds in the zoo, especially the really bright, colorful ones.
>
> Aaron: Me, too. Oh . . . what were you saying about a movie?

Remember when we talked about your "train of thought"? Sometimes your train of thought can get off track. Getting off track may be fine when you're talking, but it doesn't work very well in writing. This lesson will give you some tips to help you write clear, well-organized essays that stay on track.

TIP 1: Stick to the topic.

When you write, you must stick to the topic. The **topic** is the main subject you are writing about. Every paragraph you write should help your reader understand your topic.

TIP 2: Use topic sentences.

A **topic sentence** tells the main idea of a paragraph. Use topic sentences to help your reader understand the main point of each paragraph. When you're ready to move on to a different point, start a new paragraph.

Also, make sure to indent each paragraph. To **indent** is to start the first sentence several spaces to the right. If you are writing with a computer, press the tab key to indent a paragraph.

Read the following paragraph, then answer Numbers 1 and 2. The topic of the paragraph is mosquito stings.

> Mosquitoes don't really bite; they sting. They don't have teeth and jaws like dogs. Dogs make good pets. Mosquitoes act like a nurse giving a shot. I had a shot one time when I was sick. It wasn't too bad. First, a mosquito spits out a substance that deadens a person's skin for a few seconds. Then it inserts a very fine, needle-like stinger into the skin. Through its stinger, a mosquito draws a tiny bit of blood from its victim.

1. Circle the topic sentence.

2. Cross out any sentences that don't tell about mosquito stings.

TIP 3: Use details to support the topic.

Just as a house needs walls to support the roof, your writing needs details to support the topic. This is true in all kinds of writing—whether you are writing an informational report, a story, a persuasive letter, and so on. Here is an example:

Liz is writing a letter to the editor of her local newspaper. She wants to give her opinion about whether students should wear uniforms. Read the first draft of her letter.

Dear Editor,

I think that school uniforms are a good idea. I hope the school board will decide we should wear them.

Sincerely,

Liz Barbour

We know Liz thinks that uniforms are a good idea. But why? Liz needs to tell us why she thinks uniforms are a good idea. Some reasons she might give are found on the following page.

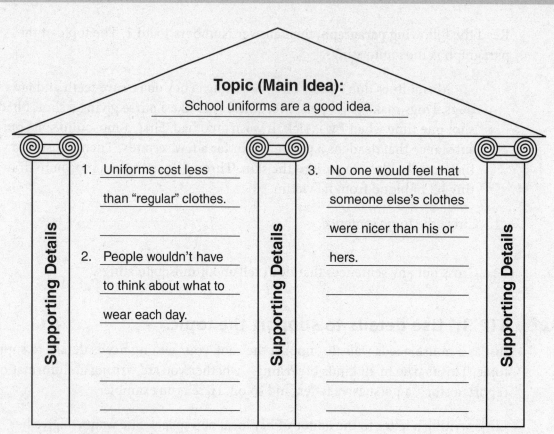

Topic (Main Idea):
School uniforms are a good idea.

Supporting Details

1. Uniforms cost less than "regular" clothes.

2. People wouldn't have to think about what to wear each day.

Supporting Details

Supporting Details

3. No one would feel that someone else's clothes were nicer than his or hers.

If Liz includes these reasons, her letter will be much stronger, and her opinion will carry a lot more weight.

Remember, your writing should have a beginning, a middle, and an end. The main idea of your essay is the most important thing you want to say. It should be stated in the beginning. Support the main idea with details in the middle section. The ending should briefly repeat your main point and give a conclusion.

 TIP 4: Give your writing a voice.

Just as you have a speaking voice, you also have a writing voice. No matter who you're writing for, your special voice should shine through. Show off your personality in your writing. Write your ideas down in a way that really shows how you feel or think about your topic.

CCSs: W.4.4, L.4.3c

 TIP 5: Know when to use formal language.

A big part of writing is knowing what kind of language to use and when. Use formal language for adults and for people you don't know well. **Formal language** is polite. It's also more "school-like." You might use formal language when writing reports and essays for school. You might read formal language in encyclopedias, newspapers, and more.

TIP 6: Know when to use casual language.

Casual language is another way of saying "everyday language." You use casual language when writing to someone you know well. When you write using everyday language, the words might come out easily. You're writing the same way you would speak. Casual language is perfect for writing for yourself, writing to a friend, or sending an e-mail to your cousin. It's also perfect for telling stories. That's because in stories, you want your characters to talk and sound like real-life people. Look at this chart. It shows the formal and casual way of relaying the same idea.

Formal Language	Casual Language
Hello	What's up?
Excellent	Awesome
You are welcome	No problem
Uninteresting	Lame

Practice Activity 1

Directions: Rewrite the sentences that follow. Change the casual language into more formal language.

1. Nicole really <u>screwed up</u> when she forgot to call her grandma on her birthday.

_____

_____

2. Some kids from my neighborhood <u>hang out</u> at City Park after school.

_____

_____

3. We saw a <u>sweet</u> magic show last winter.

_____

_____

4. <u>Chill</u>, Ross! Losing at checkers is <u>no big deal</u>.

_____

_____

5. There's something about that TV show that <u>bugs</u> me.

_____

_____

CCSs: W.4.4, L.4.3a, L.4.3b

TIP 7: Use clear and colorful words.

The words you choose are the building blocks of your writing. Some words will make your writing stronger. If the words you use are plain and dull, try using words that are more interesting instead. They should clearly describe what is happening. They should also fit the topic you are writing about. In other words, the words should be colorful. Why use *walk* when you could say *stroll*, *trudge*, or even *mosey*? Remember, you want readers to enjoy what you say.

Read the following sentence.

> The girl yelled from the sidelines as the team earned the points.

These words are not very clear. Is the girl happy or angry? What sport is she watching? Now, read the revised sentence and notice the word choice.

> The girl yelled excitedly from the sidelines as the team scored a touchdown.

The word *excitedly* tells you that the girl is happy. She must like the team that made the points. The word *scored* is a better fit for this scene. The writer also changed *points* to *touchdown*. It is clearer than *points*, and it shows that the girl is at a football game.

TIP 8: Use punctuation for effect.

You know that a period belongs at the end of a sentence. You also know that a question always end with a question mark. Did you know that there are creative ways to use punctuation in your writing, too? You can use punctuation to help readers imagine your voice. Exclamation points can show excitement or anger. Periods show a calmer tone.

The way you punctuate sentences helps readers know how your writing should be read. The following are examples of different types of punctuation and how you can use them in your writing.

- An **ellipsis** (. . .) shows a thought trailing off. In a story, a character might begin to speak without knowing what he or she wants to say. In a nonfiction essay, you can use an ellipsis to show that you are borrowing only part of an author's words.

  "I'm so sleepy, I could just . . .," Becca muttered.

  Martin Luther King, Jr., said, "I have a dream that my . . . children will one day live in a nation where they will not be judged by the color of their skin. . . ."

161

• A **dash** (—) shows that someone has stopped in the middle of a thought. It can also show that the writer is interrupting a thought, or that a person who is speaking is being interrupted by another speaker.

Students have been doing homework—or not doing it—for centuries.

"But Mom, I didn't—"

You'll learn more about punctuation in Lesson 22.

TIP 9: Connect your ideas, and place your sentences in a clear order.

Some beginning writers use one short sentence after another. They never connect those sentences in a way that makes them easy to understand.

Read the following paragraph. Think about how the writer might have organized it differently.

> David walked to school. Mike walked to school with David. It was Friday. They talked all the way. They talked about what to do on Saturday. Mike had basketball practice on Saturday. David wanted Mike to go with him to the movies. David wanted to go on Saturday. David said he had to give his dog a bath on Saturday morning. Mike said he could go in the afternoon. He would be done with basketball practice at one o'clock. Basketball is played with a ball and a net. David wanted to see a new action movie. The movie had just opened at the Astro Theater.

This is not an example of good writing. The paragraph is difficult to read. The sentences are not arranged in a clear order, which makes the ideas hard to follow. The sentences are not connected to one another, either. Some information is not needed.

3. Now rewrite the paragraph. You may put sentences together, remove sentences, and move sentences around. Be sure the general meaning of the paragraph is the same.

_____

_____

_____

_____

_____

_____

Now read the paragraph below. The paragraph you wrote may be similar.

> As David and Mike walked to school on Friday, they talked about what they were going to do on Saturday. Even though David had some chores to do, including giving his dog a bath, he wanted Mike to go with him to the movies. David wanted to see a new action movie that had just opened at the Astro Theater. Mike said he could go in the afternoon, because he would be done with basketball practice at one o'clock.

Notice how the writer put sentences together and moved them around. The writer also added and deleted words to make the meaning of the paragraph clearer.

TIP 10: Use words and phrases to connect your sentences.

When you connect sentences, you show your reader how your ideas fit together. This helps the reader follow your thoughts. Paragraphs in your writing should not be difficult to read. Ideas should flow clearly from one paragraph to another. To make your writing easy to read, arrange sentences in an order that makes sense. Use words and phrases to transition between sentences and paragraphs. A few examples of words and phrases you can use to improve your writing.

- **To add more facts** – also, again, another, next, to begin with

- **To compare things that are similar** – also, like, as, in the same way

- **To contrast things** – but, although, despite, even though, however, instead, yet

- **To identify a place** – above, below, beyond, nearby, opposite, under, there

- **To emphasize a point** – in fact, indeed, of course, certainly

- **To repeat an important point** – all of this means, in other words, to conclude

- **To give an example** – for example, in particular, a few of these are

- **To give the cause or result of something** – as a result, because, for this reason, obviously, so, therefore

- **To identify the time** – after, as soon as, before, finally, later, next, now, then, until, when, while, afterward

Practice Activity 2

Directions: Read the following paragraph. Then rewrite the paragraph so that it makes more sense. Connect your sentences using the words and phrases you learned in Tip 10. Be sure to arrange your sentences so the reader can follow your ideas. You may add or subtract words to make the paragraph clearer.

I am going to be busy this summer. I am playing on a soccer team. I am taking music lessons. I play the piano. The lessons are every Saturday morning. I am going to take care of my neighbors' pets. I want to make $25 a week. My family is planning a vacation. We are going to the Silver River State Park. We are going for a week. It will be the last week in July. There is camping. The park has hiking trails. We are staying in cabins. My best friend is going with us. Her name is Mira.

Lesson Practice begins on the following page.

Drafting

In Lesson 12, you brainstormed, did some freewriting, and outlined an essay for the following prompt:

Imagine that your class has been chosen to make a short video about your school. Students in other countries will watch it. It will teach them about American schools. You decide to write a letter to your classmates explaining what should be in the video.

For this Lesson Practice, you will write a draft of your letter. Review the Writer's Checklist, and write your draft on the lines provided. Use the notes from planning on pages 153–155 to help you write and organize your draft.

Writer's Checklist

✔ **A well-written draft:**

☐ addresses the task, purpose, and audience

☐ stays on topic

☐ uses topic sentences to begin paragraphs

☐ includes details that support the topic

☐ is written in my own voice

☐ uses colorful words and language that suits my audience

☐ uses pronunciation for effect

☐ connects ideas and connects sentences in logical order

☐ shows clear organization

☐ has a beginning, middle, and end

Directions: Write your draft on the lines that follow.

_____

_____

_____

_____

_____

_____

_____

_____

_____

_____

_____

_____

_____

_____

_____

_____

_____

_____

_____

_____

_____

_____

Lesson 14: Revising, Editing, and Publishing

You've gathered your ideas. You've organized them. You've put them down on paper. Now you're done, right?

WRONG! The best writers don't stop there. After they've written what they wanted to say, they go back and revise their work. They want to make sure their writing is the best it can be.

Revising

Revising means making sure your ideas are clear and complete. Do all the parts fit together well? Have you put in anything extra that makes your writing hard to follow? Does your word choice fit your audience?

When you revise your work, you may want to do one or more of the following things:

- add words or sentences
- combine words or sentences
- subtract words or sentences
- move words or sentences
- change words or sentences

The following tips will help you revise your draft.

TIP 1: Make sure that every sentence in a paragraph is about its main idea.

It is important that every sentence in a paragraph is about the main idea. If your sentences do not support the main idea, people will become confused as they read your essay. When you revise, watch out for sentences that don't belong.

Read the following example. It will show you what happens when the sentences in a paragraph don't relate to the main idea.

Mrs. Torres asked her students to write an essay telling about something they did during their summer vacation. Here is the first paragraph of Carlito's essay about his summer vacation.

> Last summer, my family went to the Grand Canyon on vacation. I wanted to go to Yellowstone National Park, but I was outvoted 3 to 1. When we first saw the Grand Canyon, we couldn't believe how deep it was. I dug a hole in my backyard once, but it wasn't as deep as the Grand Canyon. We signed up for a tour that took us up in a helicopter to see the canyon up close. I am going to learn how to fly a helicopter in a few years.

What's wrong with this paragraph? Carlito seems to want to talk about what he did on his summer vacation, but he keeps getting off the subject. That makes his writing hard to follow. Carlito's assignment was to write an essay about what he did on his summer vacation. His first paragraph had a problem, though. It had extra sentences that didn't have much to do with his topic.

Read the following paragraph, taken from Patricia's essay about a place she visited on her summer vacation. Cross out any sentences that don't belong.

(1) My family and I visited the Delta Blues Museum. (2) In July, we traveled by car from Biloxi to Clarksville. (3) It was a long drive, but that was okay. (4) When we got there, my brother and I were so hungry. (5) Inside the museum there were lots of different things to look at. (6) They have a big collection of musical instruments, pictures, music recordings, and costumes. (7) I like dressing up in costumes. (8) One of my favorite parts was the statue of Muddy Waters. (9) He was sitting on a chair with a 1950s guitar. (10) If you like blues music, you should visit the Delta Blues Museum.

1. Write the numbers of your crossed-out sentences on the following line.

_____

Try rereading the paragraph, skipping the crossed-out sentences. You should see that it's clearer and makes more sense.

TIP 2:   If you add something to your writing, put it where it fits best.

After writing the paragraph about Delta Blues Museum, Patricia remembered that she wanted to tell her readers to be sure to see B. B. King's guitar. Should she just tack a sentence onto the end of the paragraph? Or is there a better place to put it?

You don't want your readers to be confused or to wonder what you are talking about. So when you put your ideas together, make sure they fit in a way that makes sense. There *is* a better place for Patricia to put her sentence about B. B. King's guitar.

2.   Where is the best place for Patricia to put the following sentence?

Be sure to visit the section with B. B. King's guitar, too.

A.   after sentence 1

B.   after sentence 2

C.   after sentence 5

D.   after sentence 9

TIP 3:   Don't be afraid to change or move words and sentences.

Even the best writers revise their work. They aren't afraid to make changes. They may decide to make two sentences into one or split a long sentence in two. They may think of a more interesting way to say something. Or they may just want to rearrange their writing so that it will be clear to their readers. Sometimes they even have spelling, grammar, punctuation, or capitalization mistakes to fix.

Here's another paragraph from Patricia's essay.

(1) My favorite part of our trip, besides being away from home, was meeting Jimmy Burns. (2) He came to the museum to play and talk about his life as a blues artist. (3) He used to live in Mississippi. (4) Now he lives in Chicago, Illinois. (5) It was cool to meet a real musician.

3.   What word or words should be taken out of sentence 1 to improve it?

A.   My favorite part

B.   our trip

C.   meeting Jimmy

D.   besides being away from home

4. What is the best way to combine sentences 3 and 4?

   A. Now he lives in Chicago, Illinois, he used to live in Mississippi.

   B. He used to live in Mississippi, but now he lives in Chicago, which is in Illinois.

   C. He used to live in Mississippi, but now he lives in Chicago, Illinois.

   D. Now he lives in Chicago, he used to live in Mississippi, Chicago is in Illinois.

Remember, your combined sentence should follow all the rules of grammar.

Here's the basic rule for revising: If you're sure a change would improve your essay, make it. Essays that are carefully revised are almost always better than essays that are simply written down and handed in.

TIP 4: Use details that excite the senses.

Another way to make your writing clearer is to add details that help readers imagine the scene. Don't limit your writing to what you can see and hear. Use words that help readers taste, touch, and smell. Make them shiver in the cold night air. Let them drink the sweet, tangy juice of fresh oranges. Make them hold their nose as they take out the stinky garbage.

These details make your writing more interesting and fun to read. As you revise your draft, look for places where you can add these details.

Rewrite the following sentences by using more descriptive words.

5. Jessica put her book on the table.

   _____

   _____

6. Jared could smell something in the oven.

   _____

   _____

7. The neighbor's dog made noise all night.

   _____

   _____

TIP 5: Review the decisions you made while drafting.

In Lessons 12 and 13, you learned many tips for doing your best writing. You learned to decide why you were writing and to consider who would read your work. You learned to stick to the topic and put your ideas in order. As you revise, remember what you decided and make sure you followed through. Ask yourself the following questions:

- Does my writing address the right audience?

- Does my writing achieve the purpose I wanted it to?

- Does my writing have a main idea supported by details?

- Is there a beginning, a middle, and an end?

- Does each idea lead to the next in a way that makes sense?

If you answered *no* to any of these questions, you should revise your writing.

Editing and Proofreading

Now, you may think that after you have planned, drafted, and revised your writing, you are done. However, you still need to edit and proofread your work. The following tips will help you with this stage of writing.

 ## TIP 6: Always edit and proofread your work.

Editing and proofreading polish your writing so that errors don't confuse your readers. **Editing** is the process of correcting errors in grammar, capitalization, punctuation, and spelling.

When editing, ask, "Are there any misspelled words? Are there any words that should be capitalized? Did I leave out any commas?" Check to make sure that all grammar, capitalization, punctuation, and spelling is perfect. (Unit 3 will provide more tips about grammar, capitalization, punctuation, and spelling.)

When you are done editing, you are ready to write a second draft. This draft includes all the edits you made. Then you proofread. **Proofreading** means checking your work one last time to make sure it is the best it can be. You should read you draft through to make sure there are no mistakes. Also make sure that your final copy is in your neatest handwriting. Your reader should have no difficulty understanding what you have written.

CCS: W.4.5

TIP 7: Use the right tools to edit and proofread your writing.

The following symbols will help you mark the changes you want to make in your writing.

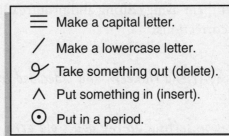

```
≡   Make a capital letter.
/   Make a lowercase letter.
ℒ   Take something out (delete).
∧   Put something in (insert).
⊙   Put in a period.
```

Here is an example of the symbols at work.

> ### My First Day at Camp
>
> At first i̲ thought that camp wasn't what it was cracked ∧to *up*
> be. e̲verything was fine through supper and sing-along, but at bedtime,
> things began to get awful. I forgot my toothbrush, ∕My roommate had
> not yet arrived, and I wished I hadn't felt too old to bring my teddy
> bear, snuggles. I was about as ~~sad~~ as a 10 year old could be until the *gloomy*
> counselor and my roommate came in together. w̲e laughed for a long
> time, ∕And I knew the rest of the week would be as good as i̲ had
> imagined. ~~Then I was happy.~~

Practice Activity

Directions: Read the paragraph Jake wrote about camping in his backyard. The paragraph has five mistakes in capitalization, punctuation, and grammar. Find the five mistakes and correct them using editing and proofreading marks. Then, rewrite the paragraph with the corrections.

One summer day, my friend Hakeem and I decided to camp out in my backyard.

We spend the afternoon setting up my dad's old army tent. we brought a bunch of peanut, butter sandwiches and comic books. As darkness came. we lay on top of our sleeping bags telling ghost stories. Hakeem says his stories were scarier I think mine were. Before long, we both fell asleep.

_____

_____

_____

_____

_____

_____

CCSs: W.4.5, W.4.6

TIP 8: Have someone else read your work.

After you have revised and edited your writing, it's a good idea to show it to someone else. Try trading with a classmate and reading each other's writing. Type up your writing and e-mail it to a friend. Or ask an adult to help you find a Web site where you can share your work. Other students from all over can send you feedback over the Internet. Another person can look at your writing with "fresh eyes." In other words, your friend may see things you have missed.

When you read another student's work, be helpful. If you see problems, point them out kindly. Be sure to say what you liked, as well as what needs more work. Never be rude.

When someone else reads your work, keep an open mind. Listen to what your classmate says. If the student points out errors, fix them. Try not to argue. If you disagree, ask a teacher to help you decide what to change.

You can also ask your teacher to read your first draft. Teachers can often suggest ways you can make your writing better. If you are writing for school, make sure you ask for help *before* the final draft is due!

TIP 9: Use a checklist to make sure your writing is perfect.

After you've fixed the errors that stood out, use a checklist to improve your writing even more. A **checklist** is a list of things to look at before you finish a writing assignment. A checklist can help you find changes that need to be made. You have already used checklists in the Lesson Practice sections of Lesson 12 and Lesson 13.

TIP 10: Publish your writing.

After you have revised, edited, and proofread your writing, why not share it? **Publishing** is printing your writing for others to read. There are many places to be published, including magazines, Web sites, or books you make yourself. Type your finished writing on a computer. Then you can print it out or send it to a publisher. Here are some ideas for sharing your writing.

- Send your writing to a magazine or Web site. Have an adult help you find and contact a publication about handing in your writing. Also, local newspapers often have writing contests. Don't just send in your writing, though. First, be sure you understand what the magazine, Web site, or newspaper expects.

- Make a book. Use poster board, cardboard, or a binder to make your writing into a book. Add pictures that show the action in your story or provide more information in an essay.

Lesson Practice begins on the following page.

Revising, Editing, and Publishing

Read through the letter draft you wrote on pages 166 and 167. Revise and edit your draft and write the final copy on the following pages. Use the checklist below to help you revise and edit. You may also want to review your planning from Lesson 12 on pages 153–155.

After you write your draft, trade workbooks with a classmate. Proofread your classmate's draft. Think about the points in the Writer's Checklist. Use editing symbols to mark corrections to grammar, capitalization, punctuation, and spelling. Then talk about the draft with the author. Your discussion should help your classmate improve the draft.

The prompt has been reprinted below.

Imagine that your class has been chosen to make a short video about your school. Students in other countries will watch it. It will teach them about American schools. You decide to write a letter to your classmates explaining what should be in the video.

Writer's Checklist

✓ **A well-written final draft:**

☐ addresses the task, purpose, and audience

☐ has sentences in each paragraph that are about the main idea

☐ uses details that excite the senses

☐ shows clear organization

☐ uses correct grammar, spelling, punctuation, capitalization, and sentence structure

☐ has a beginning, middle, and end

☐ is published for others to read using technology

Directions: Write your final copy on the lines below.

_____

_____

_____

_____

_____

_____

_____

_____

_____

_____

_____

_____

_____

_____

_____

_____

_____

CCS: W.4.1a

Lesson 15: Writing Opinions

Charlie and Tom are best friends. They love to make funny videos together. This summer, they want to go to acting camp. Their parents tell them to put their reasons in writing. "Persuade us," they say. Here is Charlie's note to his parents:

> Dear Mom and Pop,
>
>   Tom and I want to go to the Make Me Laugh acting camp this summer. You have to let me go, or else I will cry like a baby! Besides, Tom's folks already said he could go.
>
> Your favorite kid,
>
> Charlie

Do you think this note will work? It doesn't give Charlie's parents any real reasons he should go to acting camp. It looks like Charlie needs a lesson in how to persuade.

To **persuade** means to get someone to agree with you. Opinion writing does the same thing. It must include facts to support your position. It also must explain how those facts are important.

If Charlie had read the following tips before writing his letter, he might have done a better job of persuading his parents.

TIP 1: Clearly state the reason you are writing.

If you want your reader to think a certain way, say so. A clear message is more likely to persuade readers. If your ideas are not clear, you might never win your readers over.

Say what you think about the topic, and then explain why you think that way. Tell readers what ought to be done, and then explain what may happen if it is done. Show that you are sure your ideas are right. Don't make readers guess what you want; just come right out and say it.

TIP 2: Present information that supports your views.

Give your readers reasons to agree with you. Include at least three facts or examples that support your ideas. Mention an article that proves your point. Add a quotation from someone who knows about the topic. Then tell about an opposing argument. Show how your argument is better than the other. Remember to give credit to the people or writing you're borrowing from. If you have facts that support your argument, people will probably agree with you.

At the same time, leave out ideas that don't belong. If you want people to come to the school carnival, don't write about your favorite candy. Stick to information that shows the carnival is a good idea.

 ## TIP 3: Use words and phrases to link your sentences.

Link your sentences to show how one detail goes with another. Linking ideas makes your writing more organized. It helps your readers understand your ideas. Use linking words like the ones shown. They show how details go together to make your case.

Here are some of these linking words and what they do.

Linking Words and Phrases	What They Do
also, another, in addition, next	to add more facts
for example, for instance, in particular	to give an example
as a result, for this reason, so, then, therefore	to show cause and effect
also, like, as, in the same way	to compare things
but, although, despite, even though, however, instead, yet	to contrast things
in fact, indeed, of course, certainly	to show what is important
all of this means, in other words, to conclude	to repeat a point

Try using these words and phrases whenever you write. The more you practice, the easier it will be to connect your ideas.

TIP 4: Wrap up your work with a strong conclusion.

The final paragraph is your last chance to win over the audience. It should be strongly worded and bring all of your arguments together. Briefly list your main points again.

After you make your argument, remind readers what you want. Summarize the main points in your argument. If you want your readers to take an action, encourage them to do so.

Imagine you have just argued for a new city park. Next, you must tell readers what they can do to help. It could be going to a city meeting, writing a letter, or voting. Telling readers what to do next is a **call to action.** It's a great way to end your paper.

Finally, write a concluding statement. The last sentence should boil your case down to a single statement.

The following paragraph shows an example of a strong conclusion.

> A new park is clearly a good use of the city's money. It will make the neighborhood more beautiful. It will give children a safe place to play. And it will provide people a place to gather in the fresh air. Let the city council know what the people want. Come and speak at their meeting on August 1. Together, we can make a wonderful park for everyone to share.

Practice Activity

Directions: Read Tom's letter to his parents, and answer the questions that follow.

Dear Mom and Dad,

When we talked about Make Me Laugh acting camp last night, you weren't sure it was a good idea. I'd really like you to know the reasons Charlie and I want to go.

First of all, summer gets long and boring. Kids need something to do so we don't just sit around playing video games all day. Some kids even get into trouble when they don't have something to do for a whole week. (Not me, of course!) Camp would keep me busy for a week.

Second, acting camp will teach us a lot. There will be lessons on juggling, tumbling, and singing. We will read famous plays and learn how to build sets. We will be taught many skills you just don't learn at school.

This camp will also be healthy. Do you want me to spend my summer eating junk food in front of the TV? At camp, I'll have good meals and stay active. Tumbling, dancing, and swordfighting classes will give me exercise. (Yes, they really have swordfighting!)

Also, at camp I'll meet lots of interesting people. There are actors and teachers, plus campers from all over. The camp takes kids from ages ten to sixteen, so I'll have lots of good role models.

So, you can see that sending me to acting camp is a really good idea. It will give me something to do with my time, teach me lots of new skills, keep me healthy, and introduce me to some cool people. Please sign the form and mail it in today.

I won't forget this, Mom and Dad. When I win the World Acting Award, I'll thank you first. Plus, I'll write to you from camp and tell you all about it.

Your loving son,

Tom

1. What does Tom want his parents to do?

_____

_____

_____

2. What facts does Tom use to support his position? First, go back and underline them in the letter. Then sum them up here.

   a. Paragraph 2: _____

   _____

   b. Paragraph 3: _____

   _____

   c. Paragraph 4: _____

   _____

   d. Paragraph 5: _____

   _____

Lesson Practice begins on the following page.

Opinion Essay Prompt

A former student has donated money to your school. Students have been asked to help decide how to spend it. They must choose between new computers and new playground equipment.

Write an essay to persuade your principal to make the choice you want. Give at least three reasons to support your view. Review the Writer's Checklist on this page. Then, use page 185 to plan your essay. Finally, write your essay on pages 186 and 187.

Writer's Checklist

✓ **A well-written opinion essay:**

☐ introduces a topic clearly

☐ states an opinion

☐ supports the opinion with details and facts

☐ uses words and phrases to link ideas

☐ has a strong conclusion

☐ uses correct grammar, spelling, punctuation, capitalization, and sentence structure

☐ stays on topic

☐ has a beginning, middle, and end

Planning Page

Directions: Plan your essay in the space provided. You may use one of the methods for planning that you learned about in Lesson 12.

Directions: Write your essay on the lines that follow.

_____

_____

_____

_____

_____

_____

_____

_____

_____

_____

_____

_____

_____

_____

_____

_____

_____

_____

_____

_____

_____

_____

_____

_____

_____

_____

_____

_____

_____

_____

_____

_____

_____

_____

_____

_____

_____

CCS: W.4.2a

Lesson 16: Writing to Inform

Informational writing is a type of writing that gives information about a topic. When writing to inform, you will need to do research to gather facts about your topic. In your essay, your facts should be clear and easy for readers to understand.

On a writing test, you will not be able to do research. Instead, you will be asked to explain something you know about. Use the following tips to write informational essays.

TIP 1: Determine your purpose and select a topic.

The first step for writing is to decide what you want your reader to know. It is most likely that you will be given a topic to write about on a reading test. Other times, your teacher may give you a topic, or you may be told to choose your own topic. Choose one that interests you. You can even choose one you know a little about. Then ask yourself what you want your reader to know. The answer is your purpose for writing.

TIP 2: Decide how to organize your ideas.

There are many ways to organize an informational essay. Decide how your ideas go together. Group them into paragraphs. Each paragraph should explain one idea. It should contain only details that support that idea. Then give your details in the way that best explains your main idea.

Here are some of the ways an essay can be organized:

- **order of events:** Essays organized this way begin with what happens first and end with what happens last.

- **order of importance:** Essays organized this way can begin by discussing the most important points first and the least important ones last. Or the essay can start from least important and go to most important.

- **different sides of an issue:** Essays organized this way discuss ideas for or against an issue.

- **comparing and contrasting:** Essays organized this way show ways in which things are alike and different.

- **cause and effect:** Essays organized this way show why or how something happens.

- **problem and solution:** Essays organized this way start by telling what is wrong and then explain how to fix it.

- **categories:** Essays organized this way split a topic into smaller sets of things and often use headings and subheadings.

CCSs: W.4.2a, W.4.2b

You may split up your writing into sections. A **section** is a group of two or three paragraphs about the same idea. Use a heading to show where each section begins. A **heading**, like a title, should be a few words that tell what the section is about.

Before you write your draft, write an outline of your ideas. An **outline** shows the order of your ideas and how they fit together. It uses a few words to describe each section and paragraph of your writing. Imagine you are writing about types of transportation you have used. Your outline might begin like this:

I. Land vehicles

    A. Motor vehicles

        1. cars

        2. trucks

        3. buses

    B. People-powered vehicles

        1. bicycles

        2. skateboards

        3. scooters

And so on. Section II might list flying machines, and Section III might list sea vessels. You can use the section titles in your outline as headings in your essay. Each heading shows the reader you are about to discuss a new part of your topic.

 ## TIP 3: Use supporting ideas to support your main idea.

Start by putting your main idea into a single sentence. Keep the main idea in mind as you come up with good supporting ideas. It will help you stay organized and on topic.

Put each supporting idea into a sentence. These statements should form the topic sentences of your supporting paragraphs.

TIP 4: List facts and examples about each supporting idea.

For each supporting idea, list important facts and examples that support it. If you have done research about the topic, use quotations from sources. Details should be concrete; that is, about real things. Readers should feel that your ideas are based on facts, not made-up.

Give each supporting idea at least one paragraph. Write clear, focused sentences using the facts to strengthen your supporting ideas.

TIP 5: Use words and phrases to link your sentences.

As you learned in Lesson 15, you should link your sentences to show how the details go together. These linking words and phrases can show how things are alike or different. They can show how one thing causes another thing to happen. They can let readers know that more information is coming.

Here is a list of some linking words and phrases. For more, see the chart on page 180.

- **comparing:** also, like, as, in the same way
- **contrasting:** but, unlike, different, on the other hand
- **cause:** because, since, as a result of, is due to
- **effect:** therefore, thus, consequently, it follows that, if . . . then
- **adding information:** also, another, in addition, plus

Look at the following examples of linking words used in sentences. Notice how these words help ideas flow smoothly.

My family moved to America <u>because</u> my parents went to college here.

Studying music is fun, <u>plus</u> it helps students do better in math.

<u>Like</u> the Pilgrims before them, the pioneers set out to find a better life.

 TIP 6: Tell about a problem, and suggest ways to solve it.

If your topic is a problem that needs to be solved, explain how you would fix it. For example, the problem might be cheating in sports. You might suggest that anyone who is caught should not get to play again. It is up to you to come up with a way to solve the problem. Then use supporting details that show your idea will work.

 TIP 7: Use and explain special vocabulary that goes along with your subject.

You may need to use special words to discuss some subjects, such as science and math. For instance, an essay about plants may include a word such as *photosynthesis*. Using these special words shows that you know your subject. But you should always explain what they mean. (*Photosynthesis* is the way plants use light to make their food.)

CCSs: W.4.2a, W.4.2e

 ## TIP 8: Briefly review the information you have presented.

Write a concluding paragraph. First, retell the main idea. Then, go over the supporting details. Remind your readers of what they have just read. Each supporting paragraph should get its own sentence in the conclusion.

The conclusion should tie the essay together. Show how the details fit together, leading to the main idea. Then leave your readers with one final thought. It should not be a new idea that would need to be explained. The final sentence should show the reader why the essay was worth reading.

Here is an example of a concluding paragraph.

> As you have seen, each part of a bicycle is needed for it to work. The pedals turn the crank. The crank pulls the chain. The chain turns the back wheel. And the front wheel, topped with handlebars, steers and adds balance. Add a seat, and the only thing missing from the bike is you!

TIP 9: Add pictures, charts, or recordings.

Words are not the only way to give information. Support your ideas by including pictures or charts. Think about what you learned in Lesson 10. Here are some things you might add to your writing.

- **Diagrams** show how things work.
- **Photos** and **drawings** help readers imagine people or places.
- **Tables** show information quickly.
- **Graphs** show how things change or compare.

For some writing, you may be able to include sound or video recordings. You have this choice when you make a Web site. Sounds and videos are other ways to explain your topic. They can also make your writing more interesting.

Sounds include speech and music. Video clips can present a moment from history. Other videos may show how something works.

Choose pictures or recordings like any other details. They must support your ideas and stick to the topic. Remember, they should add to your writing. They do not take its place.

Lesson Practice begins on the following page.

Directions: Read the following passage about night animals. Then respond to the writing prompt.

Creatures of the Night

by Pat Covey

Most animals go to sleep at night, just as most people do. But some animals wake up when the sun is setting. They come out from their sleeping places and move around at night. Maybe you already know some types of night animals. If you have a house cat for a pet, then you're living with a night animal. Animals that sleep during the day and are awake at night are called nocturnal.

Hunters in the Darkness

Night animals can hunt in the dark because they have large eyes and wide pupils. The pupil is the dark circle in the center of the eye. Wide pupils let in more light, which helps night animals see in the dark. Some animals, such as cats, have even better night vision. Cats have a kind of mirror in their eyes. This mirror part of the eye collects more light than a human eye does. Even so, night animals usually don't see very well. They don't see shapes clearly, and they don't see colors.

Night animals use their other senses for hunting, as well. Some have a highly developed sense of smell. They can follow their noses to the animal that will be their dinner. For example, you may have noticed your cat sniffing around a hole in a wall. Neither you nor your cat can see a mouse, but the cat knows it is hidden there. The cat can smell it. Other night animals can hear especially well. Almost all bats can see, but they use sound instead of sight to tell where they're going. They make high-pitched sounds that bounce off objects. From the sound's echo, a bat can tell an object's shape, how far away it is, and where it is.

Things That Go Bump in the Night

Night animals can be mysterious. Because they rest during the day, people do not often see them. When people do hear or see night animals, the unfamiliar creatures may seem frightening. If you're outside at night, for example, you might hear a spooky wail or see a pair of glowing eyes.

Don't be scared. The wail might be a screech owl calling to its mate. The streetlight may be reflecting from its eyes, making them glow.

Night animals aren't so different from other animals. But their senses help them live in the darkness, and they have hours of adventure before the sun ever rises.

Informational Essay Prompt

Write an informational essay that explains how night animals are able to hunt in the dark. Give at least two details from the passage and one detail not mentioned in the passage (based on prior information you have heard or read about bats, owls, and other night animals).

Review the Writer's Checklist on this page. Then, use page 194 to plan your essay. Finally, write your essay on pages 195 and 196.

Writer's Checklist

✔ **A well-written essay:**

☐ has a clear purpose and topic

☐ has ideas that are grouped in paragraphs and sections

☐ includes facts, definitions, strong details, quotations, or other important information or examples about the topic

☐ uses words and phrases to link and group ideas

☐ uses special vocabulary about the topic

☐ has a strong conclusion

☐ includes illustrations and other visual elements if useful

☐ uses correct grammar, spelling, punctuation, capitalization, and sentence structure

☐ stays on topic

☐ has a clear beginning, middle, and end

Planning Page

Directions: Plan your essay in the space below. You may use one of the methods for planning that you learned about in Lesson 12.

Directions: Write your essay on the lines provided.

_____

_____

_____

_____

_____

_____

_____

_____

_____

_____

_____

_____

_____

_____

_____

_____

_____

_____

CCSs: W.4.3a, W.4.3b

Lesson 17: Narrative Writing

One day, a guy woke up, went out, came home, and went to bed.

This would be a pretty boring story, right? There are more questions than answers. Who is this "guy"? Where does he live? What happened when he went out? What kind of day did he have? Why should I care about him?

A narrative is a story. A **nonfiction narrative** is a true story. A **fictional narrative** is made-up. In either kind of story, the writer tells about the characters, what they do, and where they are. In a fictional story, the writer makes up many of those details. In this lesson, you'll learn about the kinds of things writers do to make their stories more interesting and fun.

TIP 1: Describe your characters.

Many readers want to know what characters look like, how they move, what they wear, how they feel about things, and even what their habits are. The more the author tells about a character, the more real the story becomes for the readers.

Most stories have more than one main character. Make your characters different from each other in how they speak and act. That way, your readers will be able to know them better.

1. What are some details you like to know about characters in stories you read?

_____

_____

_____

TIP 2: Describe a clear setting for the action.

Tell your readers where the action takes place. It could take place anywhere: aboard a ship, at a park, on a farm, or on the top floor of a skyscraper. Use details to help readers imagine the scene. Tell about the salty sea air and the spray of mist against the hero's cheek. Remember that our imaginations don't just see and hear; they smell, taste, and touch, too.

Also, tell your readers when the story takes place. Decide whether it is summer or winter, daytime or nighttime. It could take place anytime: now, a hundred years ago, or a thousand years in the future. Again, put your reader into the moment with details. If writing a story that takes place a hundred years ago, people in it might drive a buggy instead of a car. Let readers hear the clip-clop of horses on brick streets.

2. What other details might you include in the setting of a story?

_____

_____

 ## TIP 3: Use dialogue in your stories.

Readers like to hear characters speak for themselves. Let the characters tell the story by talking to each other. When characters talk to each other, their speech is called **dialogue**. Make sure to use quotation marks around your characters' spoken words and start a new paragraph each time the speaker changes.

Writing dialogue can be tricky. You want your characters to seem like they are really talking to each other. As you write lines for your characters, think about how they would speak if they were real. If your character is the jolly, wrinkly old man who walks with a cane, make him say the kinds of things you think jolly old men might say. Or if your character is the ten-year-old girl with the cheerful smile, she can say things ten-year-old girls you know would say.

CCSs: W.4.3a, W.4.3b

 TIP 4: Think about what will happen in your story.

The **plot** is what happens in a story. All of the events and actions of a story make up the plot. When you write a story, you need to be sure that your readers understand the sequence of events. **Sequence** means the order in which the events happen. If your reader can't tell what happened first and what happened last, the story might be hard to follow.

 TIP 5: Create a conflict to develop the characters.

Stories are built around conflict. A **conflict** is a problem a character faces. The story tells how the conflict happens. It also shows how the character deals with the problem. The conflict could be dealing with a noisy neighbor or fighting aliens from outer space. All stories must have a conflict. Otherwise, nothing would happen!

To **develop** means to grow or change. Characters who change are more interesting than characters who stay the same. As characters face conflicts, they develop. They may need to become stronger to overcome their troubles. They may learn about themselves or give up something important to them.

3. What are some kinds of story conflicts that interest you?

    _____

    _____

 TIP 6: Decide who will tell the story.

When you write a story, you need to decide who the narrator will be. From whose point of view will the story be told?

As you learned in Lesson 6, **point of view** means who is telling the story. The narrator may be a character in the story or someone outside it. A character in the story can only describe what he or she thinks, feels, hears, and sees. Someone outside it can describe the actions, feelings, and thoughts of all the characters.

It's up to you to decide who will tell the story. But once you choose a narrator, you need to tell the whole story from that point of view.

Thinking About a Fictional Narrative

Have you ever planned something and then everything went wrong? It may not have been funny at the time, but maybe you had fun telling your friends about it later. Readers enjoy stories that tell how characters find solutions to problems.

The following tips will help you write a fictional narrative.

 TIP 7: Organize what happens in your story.

Like other writing, stories must have a beginning, a middle, and an end. Before you begin writing, think about what will happen and how the story will go. You can use a beginning-middle-end chart to help you decide.

Stories mostly follow the order of events. The beginning of the story should introduce the problem and show the first events that happen. It should also introduce the main characters and the setting.

Stories use cause and effect to keep the plot moving. When you write a story, show how one event leads to the next, making the problem grow. The middle of the story should show how the characters try to deal with the problems. Don't let the characters win too easily. They should have to try a few different things before they succeed. New problems may arise.

The end of the story should show the characters facing their problems once and for all. They might not solve their problems. They may just have to live with them or learn not to make the same mistakes. But most often, the heroes get a happy ending, and that's okay.

CCS: W.4.3c

TIP 8: Use time words to show the order of events.

Readers need to understand when things happen in a story. They should know what happened first, next, and last. Mostly, you can show this by telling about events in order.

But stories are often told out of order, too. For instance, a story about a soccer game might start at kickoff. But the narrator might then go on to tell about what happened at practice the day before. This is called a flashback. A **flashback** is a scene that shows what happened before the story began.

Here are some time words and phrases that show the order of events.

- **short amounts of time:** before long, next, soon, a moment later, afterward, just then

- **longer amounts of time:** after a while, the next day, that night, the following morning

- **things happening at the same time:** at that moment, while, during, as, when

- **linking past and present:** ever since then, before, not long ago, for weeks, back then

There are other ways to play with time in your story. **Foreshadowing** is a way of hinting what will happen later in a story. The hints can be clear statements, like this:

It would not be long before Nora learned the truth.

Or the hints might be less clear:

Javier moped around the house after his best friend, Ari, moved away. He told his dad that he would never see Ari again. Dad just smiled.

In that example, Dad's smile shows readers that he probably knows something Javier doesn't. We can guess that Javier probably will see Ari again.

Link Ideas

You've learned how to link your sentences when writing opinions and informative essays. Linking words help show how one detail goes with another. You should use linking words and phrases when writing narratives, too. Use words such as *because, so,* and *since* to signal the causes of events. Words such as *therefore, then,* and *consequently* should be used to signal what happened. Compare and contrast characters and events using words such as *like, as, different,* and *unlike.*

Using these words help your readers to link ideas in the story.

TIP 9: Explain what your characters see and feel.

Details are an important part of a story. They add information about people, places, and actions. Compare these two sentences:

> Sarah heard a noise in her room that scared her.

> Sarah heard a quiet scratching noise that gave her goosebumps as she lay frozen in her bed.

Notice that adding details makes the second sentence more interesting. It tells the reader more.

As the story goes on, show what the characters see, hear, and feel. You may even explain what characters taste or smell. It all helps readers imagine what's going on. The more readers can imagine, the more involved in the story they become.

TIP 10: Tell about events.

It is important to give details about events in a story. There are many things to consider when you write about an event. How quickly does it happen? Where and when does it happen? Who is involved? What are the effects of the event? Anything you imagine about the event will help readers understand it. Use concrete words—words that show exactly what is happening. The more details you give, the more real the event seems.

Read this example of an event, and notice the details that make it seem real.

> Without warning, a large duck dove into the swimming pool. There was a loud splash as it hit the water. A storm of drops flew up around it. Screams erupted around the pool. Swimmers began to scatter away from the duck. They scrambled up ladders and heaved themselves onto the concrete. The duck let out a bunch of angry quacks. All around, people buzzed about what was going on. Finally, a little girl pointed her finger and announced, "The mama duck is getting her baby!" Sure enough, there was a duckling no one had noticed, getting an earful from its mother.

CCS: W.4.3e

TIP 11: Show that the conflict has ended in a way that makes sense.

The end of the story should show the end of the conflict. The characters are no longer struggling with their problems. Either they have solved them, or they have accepted them. That is, characters have found a way to live with things they can't change. As a writer, you need to show how the conflict has ended.

The way the conflict ends should feel right. It shouldn't come out of nowhere. For instance, if your hero is trying to climb a mountain, he or she should make it to the top or give up. Your hero should not get a ride on a helicopter that has not been mentioned before.

The ending should also be something the characters would do. Imagine you have shown a character is stubborn and sure of himself or herself. This character would not simply give up and say, "Oh, well. Maybe next time."

That doesn't mean your ending can't be surprising. But it should fit with the events that came before. A cowboy adventure should not end with a flying saucer, unless there is a reason for it in the story. For example, imagine the cowboys have been trying to figure out why their horses disappear each night. If the horses turn out to be aliens, that would be surprising. But it would still make sense in the story.

Lesson Practice begins on the following page.

Narrative Essay Prompt

Write a story about a student who must explain how he or she lost a library book. The story can be something that could really happen. Or it can be a fantasy—a story that could not really happen.

Review the Writer's Checklist on this page. Then, use page 205 to plan your story. Finally, write your story on pages 206 and 207.

Writer's Checklist

✔ **A well-written narrative:**

☐ establishes a situation

☐ has a narrator and characters

☐ clearly describes a setting

☐ is organized to show sequence of events, with a plot that unfolds clearly

☐ uses dialogue and description to develop experiences and events and to show characters' responses

☐ uses sequence words to clearly show the order of events

☐ uses words and phrases and sensory details to describe events and experiences

☐ concludes with a solution to the problem

☐ uses correct grammar, spelling, punctuation, capitalization, and sentence structure

☐ has a clear beginning, middle, and end

Planning Page

Directions: Plan your story in the space below. You may use one of the methods for planning that you learned about in Lesson 12.

Directions: Write your story on the lines provided.

_____

_____

_____

_____

_____

_____

_____

_____

_____

_____

_____

_____

_____

_____

_____

_____

CCSs: W.4.7, W.4.8

Lesson 18: Research and Information

Allison thought that her big brother Erik was cool. He was almost 18 years old, but he didn't treat her like a little kid. In fact, they hung out together.

Erik was crazy about cars. When he went off to college, Allison really missed him. Then she got an idea. She said to herself, "Erik would think it was neat if I learned about cars while he's gone. Then, the next time he comes home, I can show him what I've learned."

But where would she start? She asked her dad.

"Why don't we go to the library?" he said.

At the library, Allison and her dad asked for help. The librarian pointed them to some useful books and magazines. She also told them where to look for DVDs about cars. She provided them with some useful Internet sites where Allison could find even more information about cars.

Allison went home with a big stack of books, DVDs, magazines, and other literature about cars. *Erik is going to be surprised for sure!* she thought.

The Library's Got It

In the story, the librarian provided Allison with resources about cars. A **resource** is something that can give you information. Libraries and media centers have many different resources. This lesson will review the kinds of information you can find in each resource. You will also learn how to choose the best resource for your purpose.

TIP 1: Choose a topic.

The first step is to decide what you want to know about. Your choice should not be too broad. For instance, you could not really find out everything there is to know about animals, or even just dogs. Choose a more limited topic, like collies. Once you have narrowed your topic, a good place to start is an encyclopedia.

CCSs: W.4.7, W.4.8

1. Allison most likely will not find out everything there is to know about cars by the time her brother comes home for break. She might want to focus on a more limited topic. What topic could she focus on?

_____

TIP 2: An encyclopedia tells a little bit about almost everything.

An **encyclopedia** contains articles about many topics. The articles can be very short or very long. Often, encyclopedia articles have drawings, diagrams, maps, and photographs to help explain the topic. The topics are arranged in alphabetical order.

Some encyclopedias have many volumes and cover information about almost every subject you could think of. *The World Book* is an example of this kind of encyclopedia.

A large set of encyclopedias might look something like this.

2. Using this encyclopedia set, in which volume would you find an entry for convertible cars?

   A. Vol. 1

   B. Vol. 2

   C. Vol. 3

   D. Vol. 4

Other encyclopedias cover only certain kinds of topics. Two examples are *The Encyclopedia of Winter Sports* and *The Encyclopedia of Snakes.*

If you can't get to a library, you can search encyclopedias online. There are many Web sites that have online encyclopedias. These Web sites contain articles and videos. When researching a topic, ask your teacher or school librarian for names of online encyclopedias that you can use. It's easy to find information on an encyclopedia Web site. Just type the topic of your research in the search bar, and press enter. The information you are looking for should pop up on your computer screen in seconds.

TIP 3: An almanac is a book of facts.

An **almanac** contains facts about all kinds of topics. Much of the information is in the form of lists. You can find almanacs in the reference section of the library. Almanacs can be found on the Internet, too. Many of the facts in an almanac may change from year to year. New almanacs are printed every year, so the information is fairly up-to-date.

An almanac can help you find facts such as the following:

- the number of students in U.S. schools
- the names of all the athletes in the National Baseball Hall of Fame
- a list of the fastest animals on Earth, with their speeds
- the names of crew members aboard each space shuttle mission
- a list of the 100 most popular movies of all time
- the population, size, and location of every country in the world

TIP 4: An atlas is a book of maps.

An **atlas** is filled with maps. There are many different kinds of atlases. Some show maps of a certain part of the world. Others have maps of the entire world. If your family takes a car trip across the country, you might use a road atlas.

Each map has its own key. The **key** explains symbols used on the map. It also gives the reader the map's scale. The **scale** explains what the distances on the map mean in real life. For example: *1 inch (on the map) = 5 miles (on the ground)*.

The bodies of water and landforms shown in atlases don't change from year to year. But the borders of countries sometimes change. Names of cities and countries sometimes change, too.

Use an atlas to find:

- borders between counties, states, and nations
- bodies of water, such as oceans, rivers, and lakes
- landforms such as continents, mountain ranges, and deserts
- populations of counties, cities, and nations
- detailed maps of larger cities
- airports
- state and national parks and forests
- campsites

CCSs: W.4.7, W.4.8

Atlases can be found on the Internet, too. These Web sites usually list the names of countries, continents, and so on as links that you can click on. The links lead you to maps and information about each place. Sometimes you can even click on parts of the maps to see places. For example, say you want to see a map of Illinois. On one Web site, you see a map of the United States. From there, you can click on Illinois, then see a detailed map of the state. Other Web sites include links on the maps that you can click on to see photographs of an area.

TIP 5: Magazines and newspapers have articles about all kinds of things.

Magazines are printed about all kinds of topics. They are usually printed every week or every month. Most magazines are written for a certain group of people. Sports fans, cooks, computer users, and even kids have their own magazines to read. Magazines may provide information about a topic, entertaining stories or poems, recipes, and photographs.

Newspapers tell about important day-to-day events. In the days before TV, radio, and the Internet, most people got their news from newspapers. The information in a newspaper is usually more current than information in a magazine. Most newspapers are printed daily. Daily papers usually have news from around the world. They also have news from the state and town in which they are printed.

Most magazines and newspapers have Web sites where you can find feature articles, current events, and other pieces from their most recent editions. Often these Web sites have videos that give information. However, the Web sites often limit the amount of information a person can view. For instance, many ask you to pay to see articles from older editions. If you are searching for magazine and newspaper articles for a report, you are better off using your public library, where you can view them for free.

TIP 6: Computers can help you find information on almost any topic.

As you have learned from the previous tips, many resources are now made for use with computers. Encyclopedias, dictionaries, and even atlases have been stored on discs called **CD-ROMs**. And almost any information you are looking for can be found on the Internet, also called the World Wide Web.

Let's say you don't know which Internet resource to begin with when researching a topic. You can still use a computer to search the Internet. **Search engines** help you find information on a topic. Searching for information is easy when you use a search engine. Just type in the topic you want to learn more about. The computer will look for words matching your topic and list Web sites that contain them. But be careful. The words you type in should be exactly what you are looking for. If your search words are too general, you'll get far too many results.

For example, imagine you want to learn more about state parks in your state. If you just typed the words *state park* into Google, you would get a list of about 169,000,000 results. And most of them would not be about parks in your state. But if you typed in the name of your state and the words *state park*, you would get far fewer results. You would not have to sort through information about other states' parks.

When you use the Internet, keep in mind that different sites serve different purposes. If you're doing research, you're often better off going to sites that end with *.gov*, *.org*, or *.edu*. Those Web sites are made by the government, by a professional organization, or by schools. Be careful when searching for information from Web sites that end with *.com*. These are commercial Web sites, and only certain *.com* sites provide reliable information. Be aware that some of these sites may be businesses that want to sell things. They often present only information that makes their products sound good. Web sites that end in *.com* may also be blogs. Blogs are people's personal Web sites, with short entries like diaries. Information found on a blog may not be well researched. It may be chosen to support the writer's opinion.

3. Which Web site would be best to find facts about the NASA space program?

   A. http://www.galaxykids.com

   B. http://www.nasa.gov/home

   C. http://www.astronomy.com/home

   D. http://www.starwars.com/kids/games

Don't use the Internet to get all your facts. You should also use the kinds of books and resources listed in this lesson.

CCSs: W.4.7, W.4.8

TIP 7: Textbooks are good sources of information.

Don't forget about textbooks when looking for information. Textbooks are a great place to start your research. All you need is the right textbook for the right topic. For example, an American history textbook would be a good place to find information about Powhatan, the famous Native American chief. It would give you basic facts about his life, such as important dates and events. A textbook also provides important terms and their meanings. For example, in a science textbook you can probably find the meaning of the term *photosynthesis* in a unit about plants. The word may be defined in a section of the text or in the glossary at the back of the book.

Practice Activity

Directions: Write the type of reference needed for each item. Choose from the references below.

- almanac
- atlas
- textbook
- encyclopedia
- dictionary
- newspaper

1. to find the meaning of the word *dewlap*

   _____

2. to read about yesterday's high school football game

   _____

3. to find a map of Canada

   _____

4. to find a list of every Super Bowl winner

   _____

5. to find general information about the Gulf of Mexico

   _____

CCSs: W.4.7, W.4.8

 TIP 8: Use your experiences as a resource.

If you have some experience with a topic, don't be afraid to use it. Imagine you are writing about Mount Rushmore, the carving of four presidents' faces in a mountainside. If you have visited there, you can draw on your memories. Write about what it is like to be there. Tell about things you learned from a park ranger there. Tell about things that might not be found in other sources.

Your life experience will make your writing more interesting. It will make your essay unlike anyone else's. Your voice will really come through when you can link the topic to your own life.

Using Information from Resources

Once you know where to look, it's important that you use your sources correctly. This includes quoting your sources and telling your readers where you found the information you use.

 TIP 9: Take notes from your sources.

Imagine that you have to write a report about armadillos. You found an encyclopedia article that tells all about armadillos. What do you do now? You should take notes. When you take notes, you write down the main ideas that you find in your source. Don't just copy your source word for word.

Your source might say, "Armadillos are hard-shelled mammals that are found in the southeastern United States and South America." You could write the following on different lines in your notebook:

> They are mammals.
>
> They have hard shells.
>
> They live in the southeastern United States and South America.

Your notes should make it easy for you to find the most important information about your topic.

CCSs: W.4.7, W.4.8

 TIP 10: Paraphrase and summarize what a passage is about.

When you get information from a resource, don't just copy what the resource says. Using someone else's work is cheating, and it can get you in trouble. Instead, you should paraphrase what the author says. To **paraphrase** means to put a writer's ideas into your own words. Paraphrasing helps you make sure you understand the ideas.

Here's how to paraphrase a passage. First, look for the main idea. Remember, the author may not give the main idea in a sentence. If this is the case, write your own sentence telling the main idea. If there is a main idea sentence, underline it. Then, in your own words, explain what the sentence says.

Look at the following example.

Here is a paragraph from the book *Riding the Waves* by Alex Charles.

> Only those who are strong in body, mind, and spirit will truly enjoy surfing. You have to value each of these strengths to be able to ride the board.

Here is the way one student paraphrased it.

> Not everyone will like surfing. In his book <u>Riding the Waves</u>, Alex Charles says you have to be strong in your heart and your head, not just in your body. Then you'll have what it takes to surf.

Notice that the paraphrase is about the same length as the original. A paraphrase should give all the information from the passage. It is different from a summary.

A **summary** is a short retelling of a passage. It explains the main idea and the major details. It leaves out some of the less important details. When you write a summary, use your own words.

Read the following paragraph.

> Most of the baseballs in the world are made in China. But if you go to a major league park and catch a foul, that ball didn't come from China. That's because all baseballs used in the major leagues come from one factory in Costa Rica. Each ball made there is sewn by hand. There are 1,000 people whose job it is to sew baseballs. The fastest seamstress can sew 200 baseballs each week.

Now read this summary of the paragraph.

Major league baseballs are sewn by hand in a factory in Costa Rica. Each worker makes nearly 200 balls a week.

Now it's your turn to write a paraphrase and a summary. Read the following passage, and answer the questions that follow.

Monarchs on the Move
by Betty Bishop

You've probably seen monarchs before. Their bright orange and black wings are hard to miss! Most insects sleep during the winter, but not monarchs. Instead, monarchs fly to warmer places. This is called migration. Then, when the warm weather returns, so do the monarchs. These little flyers can move thousands of miles. They go farther than any other butterfly.

When the weather gets too cold for monarchs, they gather into groups. Then, they fly all the way to Mexico. It's a long trip for the small insects. The journey can take more than two months.

These butterflies are very good at finding their way. Some groups of monarchs even stop at the same trees, year after year. They seldom get lost. They are also very smart butterflies. Some scientists believe monarchs know how to glide on the wind, like paper airplanes. This way, they don't have to flap their wings all the time.

When the winter is over, the butterflies begin their long trip home. During this time, females lay eggs. They lay their eggs on milkweed plants. The baby butterflies will eat these weeds. Milkweed is an important food for butterflies. No other insects like to eat it, so it's perfect for a monarch snack.

Sadly, the adult butterflies die at the end of their trip. However, their children grow up rapidly and take to the air! Baby butterflies grow into adults in just 15 days. The new monarchs that come from these eggs finish the last part of the journey home.

The most unusual thing about monarchs is their skill at moving. Unlike large birds, such as swans, geese, and cranes, who learn how to migrate from older birds, monarchs need no help. Without being taught, monarchs always know exactly where to go and at what time. For years, people have wondered how these little insects do so well. The insects have a secret. Somehow, every baby butterfly has a map in its brain! It knows just where it's supposed to go. This is just one of the many wonders of the monarch.

4. Paraphrase the first paragraph of this passage.

_____

_____

_____

_____

5. Write a summary of the passage. Write one or two sentences about each paragraph.

_____

_____

_____

_____

_____

_____

_____

_____

_____

TIP 11: Create an outline.

When you start writing a report, it can be very helpful to make an outline. You learned how to write an outline in Lesson 16. Remember, an **outline** puts your ideas in order and shows how they fit together. Organize your outline this way. First, list the main ideas. Under each main idea, list details to support that idea. Turn back to page 189 to see an example of an outline.

 ## TIP 12: If you do borrow an author's words, give credit.

Sometimes the way an author says something is just perfect. The writing makes a good point or presents information as clearly as possible. You might decide to include the author's words in your own writing. There are a few rules for using someone else's work.

- **Borrow as little as necessary.** A sentence or two should be enough. If you're borrowing more than that, paraphrase it.

- **Put quotation marks around the author's words.** Like dialogue in a story, another writer's ideas should appear in quotation marks to show they came from someone else. Do not change any of the author's words.

- **Give credit.** In other words, give the author's name and the book or article title. This information should appear just before or after the quotation.

Here is an example of a proper use of borrowed words.

> In her article "Monarchs on the Move," Betty Bishop writes, "Somehow, every baby butterfly has a map in its brain! It knows just where it's supposed to go."

6. Use a quotation from the article to explain why monarch butterflies don't have to flap their wings all the time.

_____

_____

_____

CCSs: W.4.7, W.4.8

 TIP 13: Tell the reader where you found your information.

When you write a report, your teacher may want you to include a bibliography. A **bibliography** is a list of sources where you found your information. For each item on the list, include the following information:

- the author's name (last name first)
- the title of the work
- the city in which the work was published
- the name of the publisher
- the year the work was published

You can find all of the information you need for a bibliography on the copyright page of a book.

Most bibliographies look like this:

Sources

Bishop, Betty. "Monarchs on the Move." *Animal Weekly*. 25 Nov. 2010: 92.

Charles, Thomas. "Monarch Butterfly." *The Encyclopedia of Bugs*. Iowa City: Colbert Publishing, 2004.

Lind, Bob. *The Elusive Butterfly*. New York: Lepidoptera Books, 1999.

There are a few different ways to create a bibliography. Each has a slightly different set of rules. Your teacher will tell you which kind of bibliography to make.

Lesson Practice begins on the following page.

Research Report Prompt

In this Lesson Practice, you will write a research report about humpback whales. Read the information in the passages on pages 221 and 222. As you read, record notes on page 223. Then, review the Writer's Checklist on this page and prepare an outline for your report on page 224. Finally, write your report on pages 225 and 226.

Writer's Checklist

✔ **A well-written report:**

☐ focuses on a narrow topic

☐ uses a variety of sources

☐ answers questions about information I need

☐ uses my own experiences when possible

☐ uses organized notes

☐ uses my own words to summarize and paraphrase information from resources

☐ provides a list of sources

☐ demonstrates knowledge about the given topic

☐ categorizes information in a way that makes sense

☐ uses correct grammar, spelling, punctuation, capitalization, and sentence structure

from
Sea Life Encyclopedia, 2009

Humpback Whales

The humpback whale is a marine mammal found in most of Earth's oceans. It is part of the baleen whale family. Baleen is a hair-like structure that hangs from the inside of the whale's upper jaw. The humpback has baleen instead of teeth. A humpback can have between 270 and 400 plates of baleen in its mouth. The baleen helps it separate water from food.

Humpback whales can grow up to 60 feet in length and weigh 40 tons. They are mostly dark gray, with a white and gray underside. The coloring on each humpback's fluke, or tail fin, is as individual as a human's fingerprint.

Humpback whales feed mostly on krill. These are tiny, shrimp-like organisms. The whales also eat other small fish, such as herring. Humpback whales feed in different ways. Like other whales, individual humpbacks will lunge after food at the surface. Another way of feeding is unique to humpback whales. It is a group effort called bubble-net feeding. It involves several whales herding small fish to the water's surface.

Male humpback whales are known to sing. They send messages to other humpback whales by making sounds called "songs" that can be heard underwater for miles. They may use these songs for mating or to communicate with other whales.

Beginning in the nineteenth century, whalers hunted humpback whales for their oil, meat, and whalebone. By the 1960s, there were only about 1,000 humpbacks left in the world's oceans. As a result, in 1964 an international ban was placed on the commercial hunting of humpback whales. Today, there are about 30,000 humpbacks on Earth. However, the species is still endangered.

adapted from
www.NOAA.gov

"Humpback Whale (Megaptera novaeangliae)"

Where Humpback Whales Live

Humpback whales are found in oceans worldwide. They are separated into groups in the North Atlantic, North Pacific, and Southern Hemisphere. They follow a seasonal migration pattern between summering and wintering areas. In the summer, humpbacks are found in northern waters such as the Gulf of Maine in the Atlantic. In the winter, they migrate to give birth and raise calves in warm waters such as those near the Hawaiian Islands in the Pacific. Out of all migrating whales, the humpback travels the farthest in the shortest amount of time. Humpbacks have been observed to travel between Alaska and Hawaii, a total of 3,000 miles, in 36 days. Only one group of humpbacks, however, is not known to migrate. These whales spend the entire year in the warm Arabian Sea.

Humpback Whale Calves

A mother whale carries its calf in the womb for about 11 months. When first born, a calf is between 13 feet and 16 feet long. It grows quickly because of the nutrients from its mother's milk. The mother swims close to her calf, often with the calf traveling on the mother's back. Males do not provide protection for or swim with calves. At between 6 and 10 months after birth, a mother begins to prepare her calf for life on its own.

Saving the Humpback Whale

People in the United States are still working to save the humpback whale. People on boats count how many humpbacks whales are in U.S. waters. Experts educate whale-watch boats and other operators on how to safely boat around whales.

Directions: Use this page to record notes about humpback whales.

_____

_____

_____

_____

_____

_____

_____

_____

_____

_____

_____

_____

_____

_____

_____

_____

_____

Practice

Directions: Create an outline for your report on the lines below.

_____

_____

_____

_____

_____

_____

_____

_____

_____

_____

_____

_____

_____

_____

_____

_____

Directions: Write your report on the lines provided.

_____

_____

_____

_____

_____

_____

_____

_____

_____

_____

_____

_____

_____

_____

_____

_____

_____

_____

CCS: W.4.9b

Lesson 19: Writing a Response

You have thoughts and feelings about everything you read. When you read an article, you might be interested or bored. You might agree or disagree with the author's views. When you read a story, you might like the characters. Or you might find the whole story unbelievable. A good story with a bad ending might annoy you. You are bound to have an opinion about any piece of writing.

Responding to a text is writing down what you think and feel about it. Just like other writing, a response needs to be organized. It needs to explain your ideas and support them with details. In a response, all the details come from the text. Responding to text makes use of your reading *and* writing skills.

Responding to Informational Text

As you know, information can come in many forms. It can be a newspaper or magazine article, a book, or a Web site. It can even be the back of a cereal box. The text might give the author's opinion. Whatever you read, it will have a main idea and details. The first step in responding is understanding what you have read.

TIP 1: Notice the main idea and important details.

When you respond to an article, first notice what it is mostly about. Decide what the subject is and what the author wants you to know about it. If the text is meant to persuade, ask yourself what the author's opinion is. Figure out what the author wants you to think or do.

TIP 2: Judge the author's work.

Once you know the main idea, don't stop there. Consider the details the author uses. Are they facts and examples, or does the author just give an opinion? Do the details really prove the author's point?

Ask yourself how well the details support the main idea. Decide whether you agree with the author's views. If you do agree, why? If not, why not? Don't settle for "I don't know." Having a solid reason will help you write about the text.

➤ TIP 3: Read the question carefully.

You will rarely be asked to respond however you want. Most often, you must answer a question about a certain part of a text. You need to know what you are being asked. Look carefully at the question, and circle the important words. These words help you decide which parts of the text to discuss. You can go back and reread that part of the text, paying closer attention.

Imagine you have read an article about George Washington's life. Here is a question you might be asked.

> The article says that Washington went back to his farm after the Revolutionary War. The defeated King George remarked, "If he does that, he will be the greatest man in the world." What did the king mean by that, and was he right?

Some of the important words in the question are "after the Revolutionary War." They tell you which section of the article to read again. You don't need to read about Washington's childhood again. You should go to the section that begins when the war ends.

➤ TIP 4: Decide on your answer, and then choose details to support it.

When you understand the question, decide on a simple answer. This will be the main idea of your response. You might not know the answer until you go back to the article. Reread the parts that talk about the subject. Then think of a sentence or two that answer the question. In the example, the simple answer might be this:

> Washington could have made himself king, but he didn't. Yes, the king was right.

Once you know the simple answer, begin planning your response. Support your ideas with facts from the passage. Make a list of the details that prove your point. Use a beginning-middle-end chart to decide how you will present your case.

CCSs: W.4.9a, W.4.9b

 TIP 5: Explain clearly where your details come from.

As you write, discuss details from the passage. Use paraphrases and quotations from the text. Explain exactly where the details are found in the passage.

There are a few ways to point readers back to the passage. Look at the underlined parts of the following examples.

<u>As the author says in the section</u> "Washington's Cherry Tree," the story was made up years later.

<u>The author states,</u> "Washington never had wooden teeth; instead, his false teeth were made from human and animal teeth."

<u>On page 39, the author writes about</u> the long winter at Valley Forge.

Readers feel you know what you are talking about when you tie your response to the text.

Responding to a Fictional Text

In many ways, responding to a story is just like writing about an article. You must understand what you have read and what you are asked. You must write clearly and support your ideas.

Read the following story. It will help you understand the rest of the tips in this lesson.

The Tent

by Lance Ryder

Luana, Carly, and I were going camping with twelve other girls. We wanted to be the first to get our tent set up. All week long, we practiced in Carly's backyard.

The night before the trip, Luana said, "Let's just practice five more times." Each time, we were a little bit faster. By the fifth time, we were all sure we would be first. We stayed overnight at Carly's house because we were leaving early in the morning.

At 7:00, my grandmother came to pick us up in her van. "Good morning," Grandma said. "You girls hop in, and I'll take you to the campground."

On the way, we talked about how much fun it would be to be the first to set up our tent. Carly said, "After we get our tent set up, let's go around and help everyone else put up theirs."

When we got to the campground, our leader and the other campers were also arriving. Grandma said, "Why don't two of you help unload the van? The other one can go choose a spot for your tent."

I found a great spot close to the lake. Then I ran back to the van to get Luana and Carly.

When I got there, they were staring open-mouthed at the pile of sleeping bags. They looked like they were in shock. I could see that Grandma was trying hard not to smile.

"Come on, you two," I said. "Grab the tent and let's go."

Carly and Luana both looked at me with frowns on their faces. "But Jen, we forgot the tent!" Carly said. "It's still standing in my backyard!"

TIP 6: Know the characters and the conflict.

The main idea of a story is what happens when characters face a conflict. If you can tell someone about the characters and what they do, you understand the story.

Questions about stories often ask you to tell about the characters. What is a certain character like? What is the character's problem in the story? Why did this character take a certain action? How does the character feel?

Other questions may deal with plot. You must explain what happened and why. It may help you to make a timeline showing how one event caused others.

CCS: W.4.9a

Answer the following questions. They will help you think about the story you just read.

1. How do the girls in the story prepare for their camping trip?

   _____

   _____

2. What happens after the girls arrive at the campground?

   _____

   _____

3. What is the main problem in the story?

   _____

   _____

 TIP 7: Take note of the setting and events.

Authors often spend as much time telling about the setting as they do the characters. Major events are shown with many details. As you read, imagine the setting. Try to picture what's going on. If you are asked about the places or actions of the story, it will be easier to remember them. Look back at the story before you write about the details.

Think about how the setting affects the story. In "The Tent," the girls practice setting up a tent because they are going to the campground. Without that setting, there is no story. The girls could camp in Carly's backyard, and they wouldn't forget the tent. Setting always shapes the events of a story.

At the same time, events keep a story moving. If the girls just sat around at home, there would be no story. What the characters do—and what happens to them—create conflicts for them to solve. You should be able to list several major events from a story, even a short one like "The Tent."

4. List four events from "The Tent." The first has been done for you.

   1. *Luana, Carly, and Jen practice setting up the tent.*

   2. _____

231

3. _____

4. _____

TIP 8: Don't just retell the story. Tell how it makes you feel.

When you respond to a story, you must do more than retell it. The point of the response is to explain how you feel. Do you like the passage? Why or why not? If you found the story funny, tell what events made you smile. If you learned something, say what you learned and why you think it's helpful.

TIP 9: Answer all parts of the question.

Like other writing, a response to a story must be organized. You must plan to answer the question fully. Some questions may have more than one part. Be sure to answer each part of the question. You might be asked to describe the setting and explain why it is important to the story. Or you might be asked to state your opinion about something and tell why you think that way. Be careful that you don't answer one part of the question and then forget to answer the other part (or parts).

Answer each part of the following question.

5. How do you think the girls feel at the beginning of the story? How do you think they feel at the end? Why?

_____

_____

_____

_____

_____

_____

_____

Lesson Practice begins on the following page.

Directions: This passage is about a boy who is snowed in. Read the passage. Then write an essay responding to the prompt that follows.

Storm

by Tiffany Carlisle

A gray dawn had begun to creep into Mario's upstairs bedroom. The room was bitterly cold, so cold that two heavy blankets and a down-filled comforter could not keep out the chill. The wind howled, rattling the windows and causing the old farmhouse to creak and moan.

The snow that had begun yesterday morning was still falling. The raging winds continued to whip it into drifts, some of which, by this time, stood five feet high among the scattered buildings of the farmstead. Power lines were down. Water pipes were frozen. There were no lights, and there was no furnace, no water, no power, no heat. Shivering, Mario pulled the covers over his head and tried to snuggle more deeply into his soft mattress. He wished it would stop snowing.

"Mario! Breakfast is ready," his mother called from the bottom of the stairs. "We don't have electricity, but the gas stove works just fine. Hurry now—before your oatmeal gets cold."

Mario struggled from beneath the weight of the covers and dressed quickly. Pulling a winter coat from his closet, he put it on and started quickly down the stairs. The house was dark and gloomy. He noticed that a blanket had been hung in the doorway that separated the kitchen from the dining room. He pushed it aside and entered the warm kitchen, which was filled with the smells of fresh-brewed coffee and frying bacon.

"Good morning, Mom and Dad. Wow, it's nice and warm in here," Mario said, pulling off his coat and draping it over a chair at the kitchen table.

"Yeah," Dad answered. "We're using the gas burners to cook and the oven to heat the room. Looks like the kitchen is going to be our home until we get some electricity."

"Here, Mario. Sit down and eat your breakfast," Mom said. She handed him a bowl of steaming oatmeal. "Do you want a couple of slices of bacon, too?" she asked. She set the milk carton and an empty glass on the table.

"Yes, please," he said while sprinkling brown sugar over his oatmeal.

Mario ate in silence as his dad fiddled with the dial on a battery-powered radio, trying to find an update on the weather. The radio buzzed and whined and whistled, but finally Dad tuned in to a station. According to the radio, the storm was supposed to continue through early afternoon and begin to clear up toward evening. Snow plows were standing by throughout the area. They would begin to clear roads at the first sign the snow was slowing down.

"Well," Dad said, "it looks like we should have power before morning. I think Mario and I better bundle up and do our morning chores. After that maybe we could play a game or something. Anybody interested in playing Monopoly?"

Mom and Mario both agreed, then Dad and Mario got ready to go feed the cattle.

When they stepped out of the house and into the teeth of the storm, they could hardly see the barn. Snow swirls stung their eyes and skin. The wind, tearing through a grove of pine trees, sent pine needles through the air like tiny darts. Dad and Mario struggled through snow drifts, sometimes sinking to their waists. Mario put his head down, pulled his hood as far forward as it would go, and tried to keep Dad in sight.

Finally reaching the barn, they were freezing cold and nearly out of breath. The cattle were sheltered in a large covered area at the west side of the barn. Mario carried bucket after bucket of shelled corn from the grain bin to the animals' feed troughs. Meanwhile, Dad grabbed an ax. He went back into the stinging snow and broke through the ice on their watering tank. This done, Mario and Dad made the painful trip back to the house.

Dad and Mario got out of their wet clothes and hung them up to dry. Then Mom fixed them each a cup of hot chocolate. After Dad and Mario drank the hot chocolate and thawed their limbs in the warm kitchen, Dad pulled the Monopoly game out of the hall closet.

They played all that afternoon. And, because Dad's lantern gave off plenty of light, they played well into the evening. Mario was starting to wish that it would keep snowing. Just then he heard the roar and crunch of a snow plow clearing the gravel road in front of their house.

A while later, Mario rolled a 12. He moved from Reading Railroad, which he had purchased for $200 during his last turn, to Electric Company. He bought it for $150. Just as he finished buying the Electric Company in the game, the lights flickered and came back on. Then the furnace kicked in. *Maybe we are saved,* he thought.

"Mario," Dad said laughing, "why didn't you buy that Electric Company this morning?"

Response to Text Prompt

In the passage "Storm," what problems does the snowstorm cause? Does it have any good effects? Explain at least two ways the snowstorm hurts or helps the characters.

Review the Writer's Checklist on this page. Then, use page 236 to plan your response. Finally, write your response on pages 237 and 238.

Writer's Checklist

✔ **A well-written response to a text:**

☐ identifies the main idea and important details

☐ states whether I agree or disagree with the author's words

☐ answers all parts of the question, using details from the passage to support my response

☐ clearly expresses my feelings about the passage

☐ uses correct grammar, spelling, punctuation, capitalization, and sentence structure

Planning Page

Directions: Plan your response in the space below. You may use one of the methods for planning that you learned about in Lesson 12.

Directions: Write your response on the lines provided.

_____

_____

_____

_____

_____

_____

_____

_____

_____

_____

_____

_____

_____

_____

_____

_____

_____

UNIT 3

Writing "crystallizes thought and thought produces action" until I read what I've written on it.

Language

Have you ever built something with your hands, such as a birdhouse or a model airplane? Even if you haven't, you can imagine how important it is to get all the parts in the right places. If you don't, the finished product won't look good. It might not even do what it is supposed to do.

The same is true when you write. Nouns, verbs, adverbs, adjectives, and other types of words are parts of language. So are punctuation marks and capital letters. If you want your writing to look good and make sense, it's important to get all of the parts in the right places.

This unit will review some important grammar rules. It will give you tips on putting together sentences. You will also review punctuation, capitalization, and spelling rules. Before you know it, you'll be writing with style.

In This Unit

Grammar and Usage

Writing Sentences

Punctuation, Capitalization, and Spelling

Lesson 20: Grammar and Usage

A piece of writing is like the birdhouse or model airplane you read about in the introduction to this unit. The parts must fit together to make it look good and work properly. In this lesson, you'll learn how to put the right words together so the reader can understand what's written. Use what you learn in the tips to improve your writing.

Pronouns

Pronouns are words that take the place of nouns. **Nouns** are words for people, places, ideas, and things. Words like *it* and *they* take the place of nouns. Different pronouns have different jobs.

TIP 1: Use relative pronouns to add information.

Relative pronouns are used to ask questions or add information. They include the following words.

    that, who, whom, whose, which, where, when, why

We use these pronouns to ask about things we don't know. You might ask, "Who wants pie?" The answer might be, "Alicia wants pie." In the question, the pronoun *who* takes the place of *Alicia*.

We also use these pronouns to add information about the subject of a sentence. Look at the following examples.

    Tuesday was the day <u>when</u> everything changed.

    Brian got to meet Stan Lee, <u>who</u> created Spider-Man.

    It was the first time <u>that</u> he knew what he wanted to be.

CCS: L.4.1d

Adjectives and Adverbs

Adjectives and adverbs are modifiers. **Modifiers** tell about other words.

 TIP 2: Adjectives tell about nouns or pronouns.

Adjectives tell what people, places, and things are like. Words that are adjectives describe nouns or pronouns. The following table lists examples of words that are adjectives.

Adjectives
color words: *blue, black, red, green*
number words: *two, ten, double, many, less*
size words: *short, tall, large, small*
shape words: *round, square, oval*

Here are some examples that show how adjectives work.

> The <u>blue</u> ocean is <u>calm</u> today.

Blue and *calm* tell about *ocean*.

> Fiona is an <u>excellent</u> swimmer.

Excellent tells what kind of swimmer Fiona is.

In the following sentences, fill in the blanks with adjectives.

1. Diandra is a/an _____ volleyball player.

2. The _____ sky was filled with _____ clouds.

3. My _____ cat is very _____.

An **adjective clause** is a group of words that tells about a noun. A clause contains both a subject and a verb. It is added to a sentence to give more information about the noun.

> The world's largest cruise ship, <u>which is called *Oasis of the Seas*</u>, sets sail tomorrow.

In this example, the pronoun *which* is the subject of the adjective clause. The clause tells about the word *cruise ship*.

TIP 3: Adverbs tell about verbs, adjectives, or other adverbs.

Verbs are words that name actions. **Adverbs** tell about how things are done. Adverbs can show where, when, and why things happen. They can also add information to adjectives or adverbs. These examples show how adverbs work.

He spoke <u>loudly</u>.

How did he speak? *Loudly*.

The campers are <u>really</u> excited.

How excited are the campers? They are *really* excited.

We walked <u>backward</u> all the way to school.

How did they walk to school? They walked *backward*.

In the following sentences, fill in the blanks with adverbs.

4. I finished my homework _____.

5. Siri swam laps across the pool _____.

6. Dexter ate his lunch _____.

7. When Jane saw the monster, she left the theater _____ rapidly.

 TIP 4: Relative adverbs introduce adjective clauses.

Like pronouns, adverbs have different jobs. **Relative adverbs** show time, place, or reason. They include the words *when*, *where*, and *why*. They are sometimes used to add an adjective clause to a sentence. As you learned, an adjective clause uses a subject and verb to add information.

Breaking his arm was the reason <u>why Jake gave up the skateboard</u>. (The clause tells about the word *reason*.)

On the morning <u>when Renata went for a swim</u>, the water was cold. (The clause tells about the word *morning*.)

The stadium <u>where the team played</u> is being torn down. (The clause tells about the word *stadium*.)

CCSs: L.4.1b, L.4.1c

Verb Tenses

Did you know that verbs can tell time? **Verbs** tell about action. They also tell when that action takes place. **Verb tense** tells you whether the verb shows the past, the present, or the future.

TIP 5: A verb's tense tells when the action happens.

- **Past tense** verbs describe actions that have already happened.

  Yesterday, I <u>baked</u> my famous spinach pies.

- **Present tense** verbs describe actions that are happening now.

  They <u>smell</u> so good, I can hardly wait to eat them.

- **Future tense** verbs describe actions that will happen in the future.

  Tomorrow, I <u>will cook</u> my green bean supreme recipe.

TIP 6: Use helping verbs to show an action in progress.

Verbs show action: *jump, fly, learn, break*. But these verbs sometimes need help to show the action is not finished. To show actions in progress, verbs need helping verbs. A **helping verb** works together with the main verb. The helping verb *to be* shows an action in progress. Read the examples below with the main verb *read*.

Louis <u>is reading</u> a new book about dragons.

The helping verb *is* is a form of *to be*. It shows that the reading has begun and has not ended.

Louis <u>was reading</u> when I saw him yesterday.

The helping verb *was* shows that the reading had already begun when the speaker saw him.

Louis can't go to the party because he <u>will be reading</u> his book tonight.

The helping verbs *will be* show that the reading continues into the future.

Practice Activity 1

Directions: Read each sentence. Then, rewrite it on the line below, using the helping verb shown. The first one has been done for you.

1. The bridge falls into the river.

   (is) *The bridge is falling into the river.* _____

2. I watch TV.

   (was) _____

3. Nelly walks to school.

   (will be) _____

4. Shayne and I plan to be astronauts.

   (were) _____

5. Raul looks for books at the library.

   (will be) _____

6. They go to Hollywood to become movie stars.

   (are) _____

TIP 7: Use helping verbs to show that an action is possible.

Some helping verbs show that an action is possible or likely to happen. These helping verbs can be combined with other helping verbs to show actions to be possible in the past, present, or future. Verbs that are combined with other helping verbs are called **modal auxiliaries**. The following words are modal auxiliary verbs.

can	could
may	must
will	would
shall	should

The modal auxiliary always comes before the verb and adverb, if present.

That movie <u>might have been</u> the best of the year. (*Might* is the modal auxiliary verb, and *have* and *been* are the helping verbs.)

As a child, Janet <u>could</u> often <u>be found</u> in the library. (*Could* is the modal auxiliary verb, *often* is the adverb, *be* is the helping verb, and *found* is the verb.)

I <u>would have liked</u> to travel to China. (*Would* is the modal auxiliary verb, *have* is the helping verb, and *liked* is the verb.)

These modal auxiliary verbs can show how the writer feels about the action. Is the action a good idea? The writer could use *should*. Does the writer feel an action is important? The word *must* could be used.

These are not the only meanings of *should* and *must*. Modal auxiliary verbs can help you create many meanings.

In the sentences that follow, circle the modal auxiliary verb that makes the most sense.

8. You (must / may) eat your vegetables if you want to be healthy.

9. After some thought, Kendra felt she (should / might) like vanilla ice cream more than chocolate ice cream.

10. This car trouble (can / could) not have come at a worse time.

TIP 8: Use prepositions to show where, when, and how things happen.

Prepositions are words that link nouns or pronouns to another part of the sentence. Prepositions usually show time, space, or position. They are small words with a big job. If we didn't have prepositions, we couldn't talk about going <u>up</u> in an airplane, what's <u>over</u> the rainbow, or what we do <u>after</u> school.

Here are some of the most common prepositions.

Prepositions		
above	for	since
after	from	through
at	in	toward
before	near	under
by	of	until
down	on	up
during	over	with

Here are two examples of sentences with prepositions.

Jasmine went <u>through</u> the museum. She went <u>with</u> her mother.

11. Combine the two sentences into one sentence using both prepositions.

_____

_____

TIP 9: Make phrases using prepositions.

A **prepositional phrase** is a group of words that act as a preposition.

There is a vampire <u>at my school</u>.

In this sentence, "at my school" tells where the vampire (the noun) is. Here are some other examples of prepositional phrases.

under the bed	from a distance
near the water	until she arrives
during the game	in the sky

Practice Activity 2

Directions: Using prepositions, make a phrase to finish each of the following sentences. Use the list of prepositions on page 246 to help you.

1. We are going to play softball _____.

2. Lucy hung Fred's picture _____.

3. I lost one of my shoes _____.

4. I found my peanut butter sandwich _____.

Lesson Practice begins on the following page.

Directions: This passage contains errors in grammar and usage. Read the passage. Then answer Numbers 1 through 5.

---

(1) Yesterday, Jaime and his dad were going <u>up the store</u> when they got a flat tire. (2) Luckily, a tow truck driver, <u>which</u> was passing by, stopped to help them. (3) The driver <u>might</u> have asked for money, but she didn't. (4) Dad was lucky because <u>him</u> had just enough money for what he needed at the store. (5) By the time Jaime and Dad reached the store, the workers <u>locking</u> the doors.

---

1. **Which of the following corrects the prepositional phrase in sentence 1?**

   A. to the store

   B. by the store

   C. over the store

   D. with the store

2. **Which of the following corrects the relative pronoun in sentence 2?**

   A. which

   B. whom

   C. who

   D. that

3. **Which of the following corrects the modal auxiliary verb in sentence 3?**

    A. would

    B. may

    C. should

    D. could

4. **Which of the following corrects the pronoun in sentence 4?**

    A. them

    B. he

    C. they

    D. his

5. **Which of the following corrects the verb in sentence 5?**

    A. were locking

    B. had locking

    C. did locking

    D. are locking

Lesson 21: Writing Sentences

The parts of a piece of writing must fit together to make it look good and work properly. In this lesson, you'll learn how to make the best possible sentences by putting the right words together.

Kinds of Sentences

Imagine you are writing a story about an astronaut landing on an unknown planet. Think about how you could tell your readers the following ideas about the planet.

- The planet was covered with thick, purple vines.

- The planet was hot and steamy.

- The planet was small.

You could write these three ideas in many different ways.

- Thick, purple vines covered the small, hot, steamy planet.

- The small planet was hot, steamy, and covered with thick, purple vines.

- Covering the small, hot, steamy planet were thick, purple vines.

You'll have more fun writing when you use different kinds of sentences. And your readers will have more fun reading, too. The following tips will help you write complete sentences.

TIP 1: A complete sentence must have two parts.

A complete sentence needs to have a subject and a predicate. In a complete sentence, the subject and predicate form one complete thought.

The **subject** of a sentence tells who or what the sentence is about. The subject can be a person, place, thing, or idea. The subject always contains a noun or pronoun.

The **predicate** tells what the subject does or is. The predicate always contains a verb.

Subject (What or Who)	Predicate (Does or Is)
My great-aunt Claudia	is 87 years old.
She	likes to zoom around in her red sports car.

Notice in the second example that the pronoun *she* takes the place of *My great-aunt Claudia*. When you replace a noun with a pronoun, the two words must match each other in number and gender.

Practice Activity 1

Directions: Read the following sentences. Decide whether the subject or the predicate is missing. If the sentence is complete, check the *Complete* box.

Sentence	What's Missing?		
	Subject	**Predicate**	**Complete**
1. My great-aunt Claudia has curly, silver-blue hair and sparkling blue eyes.	☐	☐	☐
2. Wears bright purple dresses with big yellow flowers.	☐	☐	☐
3. Her wild, floppy hats.	☐	☐	☐
4. Is good at thinking of silly things to do on a rainy day.	☐	☐	☐
5. Her favorite song is "Yankee Doodle Dandy."	☐	☐	☐

Fragments

Once upon a time there were. Three little pigs who built houses. One built a house. Out of straw. The second little pig built. His house out of sticks. The third little pig built his house. Out of bricks.

What's wrong here? Some of the sentences in this story aren't sentences at all. They're fragments. A **fragment** is an incomplete sentence. It is missing a subject or a predicate.

In writing, fragments are trouble. They can leave readers confused. Sometimes you talk in incomplete sentences with your friends, and that's just fine. When you write, however, you need to use complete sentences to be clear.

TIP 2: Fix a sentence fragment by adding either a subject or predicate.

As you have already read, a sentence needs a subject and a predicate. Without either of these, you have a fragment.

> **Fragment:** During the storm, the tree in the yard.

What happened to the tree? Notice that the example is missing a verb. Without a verb to explain what happened, there is no complete thought.

> **Complete:** During the storm, the tree in the yard <u>fell</u>.

Here's another example.

> **Fragment:** Flashed across the night sky.

What flashed across the night sky? This example does not have a subject. Without a subject to perform or receive the action of the verb, there is no complete thought.

> **Complete:** <u>Lightning</u> flashed across the night sky.

Practice Activity 2

Directions: Make the fragments into complete sentences. Write your new sentences on the lines provided.

1. The woman with an orange hat. Riding a purple bicycle.

   _____

   _____

2. Before Ahmed got his new 10-speed bike. Learn how to use it.

   _____

   _____

3. Airplane. Hummed through the midnight air.

   _____

   _____

4. I saw Tom. Flying his model airplane.

   _____

   _____

5. Mom finally said I could. Go to the mall with Rachel.

   _____

   _____

Run-On Sentences

Run-on sentences are two or more complete sentences incorrectly made into one. Look at the following examples.

My new video game is fun I think I could play it all day.

Mom says I should play ball with my brother, I don't want to because he always wins.

This last type of run-on sentence is sometimes called a **comma splice** because two sentences are linked together (spliced) with a comma.

Run-on sentences can be fixed in a couple of ways.

TIP 3: **A run–on sentence can often be broken into two complete sentences.**

Split a run-on into two sentences by adding a period after the first complete thought.

My new video game is fun. I think I could play it all day.

Mom says I should play ball with my brother. I don't want to because he always wins.

TIP 4: **Fix a run–on sentence by connecting two thoughts with a comma and a conjunction.**

Another way to correct a run-on is to use a comma and a conjunction. A **conjunction** is a word that joins one idea to another, such as the following: *and, but, or, nor, for, so,* or *yet.*

Run-on: This game is easy to learn it's hard to get to the highest level.

Correct: This game is easy to learn, but it's hard to get to the highest level.

Practice Activity 3

Directions: Label each sentence with *F* for *fragment*, *R* for *run-on*, or *C* for *complete sentence*. Rewrite each fragment or run-on to make it a complete sentence or pair of sentences. Add or take out words if needed. The first one has been done for you.

___F___ 1. Flew away in its flying saucer.

The alien flew away in its flying saucer.

_____ 2. After putting the leash on his dog, took him for a walk.

_____ 3. She did her math, science, and reading homework, after that, she went over to her friend's house to play.

_____ 4. It rained all day, so we stayed inside and did puzzles.

_____ 5. I love to go swimming Sara, however, hates to be out in the sun.

_____ 6. Although he says he does not like spinach and doesn't eat it when it's served at school.

TIP 5: Put adjectives in the right order in a sentence.

When you use more than one adjective to tell about a noun, make sure they sound right together. In English, adjectives are usually put in order by what type of word they are. For instance, you would not normally say "a red big ball." You would say "a big red ball." That is because, without even knowing it, you follow the rules of English. You know that size comes before color.

Here are the basic types of adjectives in the order they usually follow.

- **opinion** – *good, bad, funny, amazing*

  When I took off my shoes, I was surprised to see a <u>funny</u> red bump on my toe.

- **size** – *large, tiny, little, tall*

  Mom took the <u>tall</u>, blue, glass bowl out of the cabinet and set it on the table.

- **age** – *new, ancient, fresh, worn*

  Jonathan let me ride his <u>new</u> yellow bicycle to Marcy's house.

- **shape** – *round, square, star-shaped*

  Mrs. Hernandez wore a <u>star-shaped</u> purple jewel necklace.

- **color** – *red, greenish, muddy, brown*

  Rafael bounced the <u>brown</u> rubber ball off the wall.

- **origin** – *American, Martian, western, Italian*

  When Mr. Ling drove his new, red, <u>Italian</u> sports car down our block, my dad became jealous.

- **material** – *wooden, plastic, silk, metal*

  Aunt Mitzy asked me to put the flowers in the red <u>plastic</u> vase by the window.

- **purpose** – *writing, sleeping, listening*

  I told my little sister that the <u>writing</u> tablet is for creating magic letters that only elves can read, and she believed me!

CCS: L.4.1d

1. The following sentence uses a number of adjectives. Read the sentence, then circle the adjectives.

   I met this amazing little old man who sold me black Italian leather driving gloves.

Rewrite the following sentences with the adjectives in the correct order.

2. Martha laughed when Dora's plaid ugly big hat blew right off her head.

   _____

   _____

3. Jamal wears only Japanese rubber sandals in the summer and plastic worn orange boots in the winter.

   _____

   _____

4. Mrs. Chang screamed when she found a green fat toad in her mailbox.

   _____

   _____

5. The sleeping small child was tucked under a square large knit blanket.

   _____

   _____

Lesson Practice begins on the following page.

Directions: This passage contains errors in grammar and usage. Read the passage. Then answer Numbers 1 through 5.

---

(1) People like to race. (2) <u>Whether it's on foot or in a wheelchair.</u> (3) <u>The fastest runner in the world is Usain Bolt, he is from Jamaica.</u> (4) Bolt ran the 100-meter race in 9.58 seconds. (5) <u>Broke his own world record.</u> (6) In 2010, a <u>Dutch 20-year-old strong</u> wheelchair racer named Kenny van Weeghel finished a 100-meter race in 14.7 seconds. (7) <u>Women love racing as much as men their best times are a second behind the men's.</u>

---

1. **Which of the following correctly combines sentences 1 and 2?**

   A. People like to race, whether it's on foot or in a wheelchair.

   B. People like to race; whether it's on foot or in a wheelchair.

   C. People like to race, and whether it's on foot or in a wheelchair.

   D. People like to race. Whether they are on foot or in a wheelchair.

2. **Which of the following corrects the run-on in sentence 3?**

   A. The fastest runner in the world is Usain Bolt he is from Jamaica.

   B. The fastest runner in the world, Usain Bolt, he is from Jamaica.

   C. The fastest runner in the world, Usain Bolt, is from Jamaica.

   D. The fastest runner in the world. Usain Bolt, he is from Jamaica.

3. **Which of the following correctly combines sentences 4 and 5?**

    A. Bolt ran the 100-meter race in 9.58 seconds, broke his own world record.

    B. Bolt ran the 100-meter race in 9.58 seconds and broke his own world record.

    C. Bolt ran the 100-meter race in 9.58 seconds; broke his own world record.

    D. Bolt ran the 100-meter race in 9.58 seconds. Bolt broke his own world record.

4. **Which of the following corrects the adjective order in sentence 6?**

    A. In 2010, a strong 20-year-old Dutch wheelchair racer named Kenny van Weeghel finished a 100-meter race in 14.7 seconds.

    B. In 2010, a Dutch 20-year-old strong wheelchair racer named Kenny van Weeghel finished a 100-meter race in 14.7 seconds.

    C. In 2010, a 20-year-old strong Dutch wheelchair racer named Kenny van Weeghel finished a 100-meter race in 14.7 seconds.

    D. In 2010, a 20-year-old Dutch strong wheelchair racer named Kenny van Weeghel finished a 100-meter race in 14.7 seconds.

5. **Which of the following corrects the run-on in sentence 7?**

    A. Women love racing as much as men, but their best times are a second behind the men's.

    B. Women love racing as much as men; but their best times are a second behind the men's.

    C. Women love racing as much as men, their best times are a second behind the men's.

    D. Women love racing as much as men but their best times are a second behind the men's.

CCSs: L.4.2b, L.4.3b

Lesson 22: Punctuation, Capitalization, and Spelling

Imagine that you had to read this paragraph:

> a person Does not choose his brotHers And Sisters we are usually Stuck with What we get they can Be great Fun but they Also can be terRible Pests my Little brotHer mikey can be Both with mikey You never knOW what youRe Going to geT

You would probably think, *What's going on here? What's with the capital letters? Where are the punctuation marks?* If there were no rules for capital letters and punctuation, writing could get pretty weird.

When you start writing, capitals and punctuation might be the last things on your mind. But you can't just forget about them. If you use capital letters in strange ways, your writing will be difficult to read. If you don't use periods or commas, your writing might not get read at all.

So, when you are correcting your writing, check for capital letters and punctuation. The following tips will help you out.

Punctuation

The following tips will help you edit punctuation in your writing.

TIP 1: Place spoken words in quotation marks.

Quotation marks (" ") make written conversations easier to follow. When writing conversations between people, follow these rules.

- Use quotation marks around the words that people are speaking.

    "Can you watch where you're going?" Matt asked.

- Put end punctuation and a comma inside the quotation marks at the end of the person's words.

    "I didn't step in front of you," Moriah said. "You stepped in front of me."

- Each time a different person speaks, begin a new paragraph.

    "Sorry," Matt said. "I'm late for my math class."

    "That's okay," Moriah said, "as long as it doesn't happen again."

TIP 2: Use commas to introduce or follow quotations.

Writers use quotations to show words spoken by someone else. When using quotations, always use a comma to set the quotation off from the rest of the sentence.

> Scott said, "I hit the ball so hard, it turned to dust."

> "You did not," Becky said.

> "I did," Scott said, "but you didn't see it."

Here are some things to remember when using commas with quotations.

- When the comma comes before the quotation, don't put it inside the quotation mark.

- When the comma comes at the end of the quotation, do put it inside the quotation mark.

- When the quotation is broken in the middle, follow both of these rules. Put the first comma inside the quotation. Put the second comma outside the quotation.

 TIP 3: Use a comma before the conjunction in a compound sentence.

When the second part of a compound sentence starts with *and*, *but*, *nor*, *or*, *so*, *for*, and so on, use a comma before the second part. (Remember, you learned about compound sentences and conjunctions in Lesson 21.)

> I love the talent show, <u>but</u> I'm not sure what my talent is.

> My mom is from New Jersey, <u>and</u> my dad is from Puerto Rico.

Capitalization

When you are editing your writing, always check for capitalization. Here are a few tips to help you out.

 TIP 4: Capitalize the first word of each new sentence.

Capital letters begin sentences for a reason. Capitalization (along with punctuation) helps readers see that you are moving into a new thought.

> Our baseball team is doing really well this year. We haven't lost any games by more than ten runs.

 TIP 5: Capitalize people's names.

Some nouns are general. They don't tell you about any specific person, place, or thing. *Girl*, *dog*, and *writer* are general. But names are different. You need to capitalize them, just as you do your own name.

> Hannah Barnes   Bella Swan   Nemo
>
> Joey Smith   Kurt Warner   my cousin Harold

 TIP 6: Capitalize titles that go with people's names.

When you use them by themselves, you don't need to capitalize words like *doctor* or *king*. But if you put those words in front of a person's name, the title becomes a part of the name.

> Prince William   Mr. Krystal   Dr. Jane Jones
>
> President Lincoln   Captain Cook   Principal Skinner

TIP 7: Capitalize words you use in place of family members' names.

Depending on how you use them, family titles can be nouns that are used like names. If you're using the family title in place of a family member's name, use capital letters.

Mom	Grandfather
Dad	Grandma

When you're not using a family title in place of a person's name, do NOT capitalize it.

my mom	my grandfather
her dad	Jacob's aunt Bea

TIP 8: Capitalize the names of cities, states, countries, and languages.

You should always capitalize names that refer to specific places, as well as languages from those places.

Fargo	North Dakota	Japan	English
Mexico	Dutch	Vietnam	Iowan

TIP 9: Capitalize days, months, and holidays, but do not capitalize seasons.

This rule is pretty easy to remember. The biggest trick is making sure you don't capitalize the names of the seasons: winter, spring, fall, and summer.

Friday	February 14	Valentine's Day
Monday	April 1	April Fools' Day

TIP 10: Capitalize brand names.

Brand names are names companies come up with for their products. These names aren't general. They refer to specific things. Because of this, you need to capitalize those brand names.

Levi   Cheerios   Chiquita

 TIP 11: Capitalize the titles of books, movies, and songs.

Titles are like other nouns you've learned about in this lesson. They refer to something specific, not to something general.

There is one tricky part of this rule, though. Don't capitalize words such as *and*, *the*, or *of* unless they are the first word of the title. Those words aren't as important or as meaningful as the other words in a title.

How to Eat Fried Worms   "Baa Baa Black Sheep"

The Tales of Beedle the Bard   *Horton Hears a Who!*

 TIP 12: Always capitalize the word *I*.

This is probably the easiest capitalization rule of all. It never changes. Any time you have an *I* by itself as a word, capitalize it.

Today, I wrote a story about myself. I think it's the best story I have ever read.

TIP 13: Capitalize the first word of a quotation.

Quotations are often parts of other sentences. Still, you should almost always capitalize the first word of a quotation. You do this because it helps the reader see that you are shifting over to someone else's "voice."

Michael asked, "Have you seen my model skeleton?"

Practice Activity 1

Directions: Rewrite each sentence using capital letters where they are needed.

1. on monday, february 20, our country will celebrate presidents' day.

   _____

   _____

2. we will sing the song "the good ship lollipop" at the spring concert.

   _____

   _____

3. last year, mom, dad, my sister amber, and i all moved from kalamazoo, michigan, to dubuque, iowa.

   _____

   _____

4. my brother nathaniel and i searched all day long for a mother's day present.

   _____

   _____

Spelling Tools

Maybe spelling doesn't matter so much when you are first gathering your ideas. *You know what you mean to say. But will anyone else?*

Your job is to make sure that your writing is easy for others to read. Here are a few spelling tips to help you out.

Prefixes and Suffixes

You read about prefixes, suffixes, and root words in Lesson 1. Adding a prefix to the beginning of a root word or a suffix to the end is like adding a link to a chain. You simply hook the two parts together to make a new word.

Prefix	Suffix
mis + trust = mistrust	trust + ing = trusting
dis + appear = disappear	appear + ance = appearance

 TIP 14: Watch for a silent *e*.

Adding suffixes can be a bit harder because suffixes sometimes change the spelling of the root word. If the suffix begins with a **vowel** (*-able, -ible, -ion, -ing*), drop the silent *e* at the end of the word before adding the suffix.

move + able = mov<u>able</u>

If the suffix begins with a **consonant** (*-ly, -ment, -ness*), keep the silent *e*.

like + ness = like<u>ness</u>

There are some words that don't follow these rules, such as the following:

true + ly = tru<u>ly</u>

whole + ly = whol<u>ly</u>

If you're not sure, check a dictionary.

Practice Activity 2

Directions: Add the suffixes to the following words.

1. imagine + able = _____

2. hope + ful = _____

3. dare + ing = _____

4. time + less = _____

5. believe + able = _____

Directions: Add the prefixes to the following words.

6. dis + appoint = _____

7. mis + take = _____

8. un + like = _____

9. re + build = _____

10. non + sense = _____

Plurals

Plurals are words that describe more than one thing (two boys, five cats, and a dozen scratches).

 TIP 15: To form most plurals, add –*s* or –*es*.

For most words, add -*s* to form the plural.

apple + s = apples   cup + s = cups   car + s = cars

For words ending in *s*, *ss*, *ch*, or *x*, add -*es*.

dress + es = dresses   church + es = churches   tax + es = taxes

For words ending in a consonant plus the letter *y*, change the *y* to *i* and add -*es*.

fairy – y + ies = fairies   kitty – y + ies = kitties

Practice Activity 3

Directions: Make the following words into plurals.

1. book _____

2. lady _____

3. glass _____

4. puppy _____

5. lunch _____

CCS: L.4.2d

Other Tips to Remember

Now that you have reviewed the tips for suffixes and plurals, here are some more spelling tips to keep in mind.

 TIP 16: Remember the "*i* before *e*" rule.

Here's the rule for remembering the order of *i* and *e* in the same word: *I* before *e*, except after *c* or when saying *a* as in *neighbor* and *weigh*.

i before *e*	except after *c*	or when saying *a*
belief	ceiling	neighbor
niece	receive	rein

Practice Activity 4

Directions: Circle the word that is spelled correctly.

1. Pocahontas was the daughter of a Native American (cheif / chief).

2. Sharla used her coat as a (shield / sheild) against the wind.

3. Queen Elizabeth II of England has (reigned / riegned) since 1952.

4. How many (freinds / friends) are going with you to the mall?

5. Before there were cars, some people traveled by (sleigh / sliegh) in the winter.

TIP 17: Remember the rule for silent –*e* syllables.

When a silent *e* follows a consonant-vowel-consonant pattern (such as *cap* or *rip*), it makes the first vowel say its name (*cape*, *ripe*).

 ## Practice Activity 5

Directions: Circle the word that is spelled correctly.

1. Victor climbed up the steep (slop / slope) of the mountain.

2. Janet took a large (bit / bite) out of the apple.

3. Nelson's frog can (hop / hope) more than five feet at a time.

4. I want to buy a strawberry ice cream (con / cone).

TIP 18: Get to know spelling patterns.

There are many groups of words that share similar spellings. When you learn a new word, try to think of another word that is spelled like it. This will help you remember how to spell when you are sounding out words. Recognizing spelling patterns makes it much easier to think of rhyming words, too.

Look at the following spelling patterns.

ought	ight	ash
ought	right	dash
bought	bright	crash
brought	flight	splash
fought	might	flash
thought	delight	eyelash

Other spelling patterns include *ake, ame, ank, ink, ump,* and *urse.*

On the lines that follow, list two words that use the *ank* pattern.

1. _____

2. _____

➤ **TIP 19: Homophones are words that sound alike.**

Homophones are words that sound the same but have different spellings and meanings.

Where will she *wear* those torn jeans?

She can't *see* or *hear* the *sea* from *here*.

Because homophones sound the same, it's easy to accidentally use the wrong word when you are writing. You need to be careful because using the wrong homophone can change the whole meaning of a sentence.

The following are some of these tricky words to watch for.

by	The weather is fairly warm by June.
bye	Say good-bye to snowy weather.
buy	Let's rush out to buy swimsuits for the summer.
dear	Jennifer's pets are very dear to her.
deer	Her favorite is a pet deer named Bambi.
hear	Did you hear the news?
here	A dangerous storm will soon be here.
it's (it is)	It's time to feed our pet snake.
its	Last week the snake shed its skin.
meet	Would you like to meet Mr. Venison?
meat	He is the owner of the meat market.

their	Cindy and Juan left their skates outside.
they're (they are)	They're inside getting a glass of lemonade.
there	The skates are still there by the front step.

to	Are you going to the state spelling bee?
two	Two students from our school will compete.
too	They think they'll win first place, too.

Practice Activity 6

Directions: Circle the word that best fits each sentence.

1. Scientists learn about animals that lived long ago (by / bye / buy) studying fossils.

2. If Margaret could (meat / meet) anyone from the past, she would choose Mark Twain, a famous author.

3. How long does it take a space shuttle (to / too / two) circle Earth?

4. Orville and Wilbur Wright successfully flew (there / their / they're) airplane for the first time in 1903.

5. Do you know (who's / whose) going to be in the school talent show this year?

Lesson Practice begins on the following page.

Directions: This passage contains errors in punctuation, capitalization, and spelling. Read the passage. Then answer Numbers 1 through 5.

---

(1) Arthur pulled the office door handle again and again but it wouldn't budge. (2) He new it would be one of those days. (3) Just earlier, he thought about how he got off on the "wrong side of the mattress." (4) Then, when he went to get his coffee, the woman at the counter told him that he had toothpaste on his face. (5) He missed his bus, forgot his lunch, and grabbed the wrong breifcase. (6) He thought the day couldn't get any worse when he realized that it was saturday! (7) Their was no reason for him to be at work.

---

1. **Which correctly punctuates the compound sentence in sentence 1?**

    A. Arthur pulled the office door handle, again and again but it wouldn't budge.

    B. Arthur pulled the office door handle again and again. but it wouldn't budge.

    C   Arthur pulled the office door handle again and again, but it wouldn't budge.

    D. Correct as is.

2. **Which is the correct spelling of the word *new* in sentence 2?**

    A. knew

    B. gnu

    C. nu

    D. Correct as is.

3.   **Which is the correct spelling of the word *breifcase* in sentence 5?**

   A.   breivcase

   B.   brefcase

   C.   briefcase

   D.   Correct as is.

4.   **Which correctly capitalizes the word *saturday* in sentence 6?**

   A.   Saturday

   B.   saturDay

   C.   SaturdaY

   D.   Correct as is.

5.   **Which is the correct spelling of the word *Their* in sentence 7?**

   A.   There

   B.   They're

   C.   Thair

   D.   Correct as is.

UNIT 4

Speaking and Listening

Reading and writing aren't the only ways you use words. In fact, they aren't even the main ways. Most people spend their days talking and listening to each other. But there are times when you speak or listen in special ways. You often must present information to an audience. You need to make yourself understood. Even more often, you listen to get information from a speaker. There are ways to get the most from what you hear.

This unit will review skills for speaking and listening in the classroom.

In This Unit

Listening

Discussing

Speaking

Lesson 23: Listening

Shannon called her friend David. His mother answered, "Hello?"

"Hi, Mrs. Yamato. This is Shannon. Is David home?"

"No, dear," Mrs. Yamato said. "But I would be more than happy to give him a message."

Shannon knew Mrs. Yamato wasn't great about taking messages. But she decided to go for it anyway. "Please ask him to call me about our science project. It's due on Wednesday."

"A history project, you say?" Mrs. Yamato asked.

"No, Mrs. Yamato," Shannon replied, "a science project."

"And it's due on Monday?"

"No," Shannon said, "Wednesday, Mrs. Yamato. Wednesday."

"And you want him to stop over at your house?"

"No, ma'am," Shannon repeated. "He can just call. I only need to ask him one question."

"He needs to ask you a question?" David's mother asked.

"No, Mrs. Yamato. I want to ask David a question."

"Okay, Hannah. Math is so important. I'll send him right over."

Click.

Ugh!

We all have been in situations like this. Sometimes we're the speaker, and sometimes we're the listener. When you listen for information, it's important to get the message. The tips in this lesson will help you build your listening skills.

TIP 1: Listen for the main idea.

Listening is like reading. The ideas you hear are planned out. Speakers often tell a main idea and then list details about it. When a speaker begins, pay attention to the topic. Next, notice what the speaker says about the topic. Does the speech only inform? Or does it give an opinion?

It's not enough to say, "That speech was about basketball." You should be able to sum up the main idea: "The speaker explained why she thinks college basketball is more exciting than pro basketball."

CCSs: SL.4.2, SL.4.3

 TIP 2: Take brief notes, paraphrasing the speaker's words.

The best way to understand and remember a speech is to take notes. **Note-taking** is writing down important ideas from what you hear and see. Don't worry about writing complete sentences. Your notes are for you. No one else will read them. So, you only need to include words that will help you remember the speech.

Plus, putting ideas into your own words helps you understand them. As you listen, think to yourself, *So what you're saying is . . .* If you aren't sure, you may be able to ask speakers to explain what they mean.

Don't get carried away with taking notes. If you get too involved in writing, you might not listen as well. Write down only what you think is most important.

TIP 3: Notice what you see, not just what you hear.

Speakers often use pictures to help explain their ideas. The picture might be a photo, a graph, or a diagram. They may hold up an example, or prop, to illustrate what they are discussing. For example, a speaker talking about history might show an example of a piece of clothing worn long ago. Speakers may show videos, too. Some speakers show how to do something by doing it. For instance, a chef might explain how to cook while mixing ingredients.

If a speaker shows you a picture or action, ask yourself why. What does it tell you? Write a few notes about what you see. If possible, draw a sketch of what the speaker has shown you. Again, don't worry about getting your drawing just right. Include the important details you want to remember later.

TIP 4: Consider how speakers support their claims.

Speakers often do more than give information. They use their speeches to persuade audiences. They express opinions and tell how problems should be solved. Your job is to decide whether you agree or disagree.

When you hear speakers giving opinions, how can you judge those opinions? First, understand the speakers' claims. **Claims** are ideas that speakers want you to believe. They may be facts or opinions. A factual claim might look like this:

> Most dentists agree that daily flossing prevents gum disease.

This statement is a fact. You could check this claim by taking a poll of dentists. But that would be hard to check, especially while you are listening to a speech. It is up to the speaker to support this claim. Imagine the speaker goes on to say this:

> A 2010 study by the World Dental Group found that 98 percent of dentists suggest flossing every day.

This statement supports the speaker's claim. **Supporting details** show that the speaker has looked into the facts. When speakers do not support their claims, you have little reason to believe them.

Some claims are opinions, but they still need support. Read the following claim.

> Jazz is the most boring music to hear.

Clearly, not everyone would agree. But a speaker should give reasons for this opinion. If the reasons make sense, you might be more willing to listen, even if you disagree. If there are no good reasons, the rest of the argument will be weaker.

As you take notes while listening to a speech, record each claim and how it is supported. If a claim is not well supported, say so. Your notes will help you judge how good the speech was.

Lesson Practice begins on the following page.

Listening

You are going to listen to a passage called "Bicycle Safety Rules." Then you will answer some questions to show how well you understood what was read.

You will listen to the passage twice. The first time you hear the passage, listen carefully, but do not take notes. Look at the pictures below as you listen to the passage. As you listen to the passage the second time, you may want to take notes.

Use the space on page 280 for your notes. You may use these notes to answer the questions that follow.

Bicycle Safety Rules

Dos:

Right turn *Left turn* *Stop or slow*

Use hand signals.   Walk across busy streets.

Keep to the right.   Obey traffic signs.   Ride in single file.

Don'ts:

Don't do stunts.   Don't ride double.   Don't hitch rides.

Directions: Write notes on the lines below as you listen.

_____

_____

_____

_____

_____

_____

_____

_____

_____

_____

Listening Checklist

✔ **A good listener:**

☐ listens for the main idea

☐ takes brief notes

☐ paraphrases the speaker's words

☐ pays attention to illustrations

☐ identifies how the speaker supports his or her claims

1. What are two hand signals bicycle riders use, and when do they use them?

   _____

   _____

   _____

2. What are some ways to be safer while riding a bicycle? Give at least two examples.

   _____

   _____

   _____

3. The author calls bicycling "safe and inexpensive" and "fun and healthy." How well does the author support these claims? Support your answer with details from the passage.

   _____

   _____

   _____

   _____

   _____

CCS: SL.4.1a

Lesson 24: Discussing

Sometimes we are surprised by what our friends know. We can learn a lot from them. Often, we can teach them something, too. We help each other by sharing knowledge and opinions.

A **discussion** is a way for a group to share ideas. It can help people understand information. It can also help them make decisions together.

Discussions are common in classrooms. They can also take place at home or on the playground. When people need to agree on something, they often meet to discuss it.

1. Name another situation in which you would have a group discussion.

_____

A good discussion is a two-way street. Each member of the group should add something. Group members should also listen to what the others have to say. The tips in this lesson will help you actively participate in a discussion.

 ## TIP 1: Be prepared.

The best thing you can bring to a discussion is knowledge. If you are going to discuss a story, read it before hand. But don't stop there. Often, you know what a discussion is going to touch on. Think about the questions you will need to answer. Also think about questions you want to ask.

You may already know a little about a subject before you read. Think about what you can share in a discussion. For example, if you have played tennis, you can help explain the sport to those who haven't.

Make a few notes before the discussion to remind yourself of what you want to add. You can't guess everything that will be discussed, but you can be ready to share what you know.

 ## TIP 2: Be involved.

Of course, knowledge is only helpful if you share it. In a discussion, you need to make your voice heard. Don't interrupt others; wait your turn. If you have something to add, do so. If there's something you don't understand, ask the group about it. Someone else can probably answer you. If no one can, the group might be able to figure out the answer together.

CCSs: SL.4.1a, SL.4.1c, SL.4.6

When you speak, talk about the material you have read. Point to ideas in the text that support your opinions. Ask questions about the author's facts. Again, if you don't understand part of the text, ask the group. If you can help someone else understand something, offer to explain it.

If you have read more about a subject, tell what you know. You might be an expert about the subject—or at least know something your group doesn't.

TIP 3: Ask questions and answer others.

We've said it before, and we'll say it again. One way you can add to the discussion is by asking questions. You may want someone to help you understand what you've read. Or you may want others to explain what they have said. Part of a discussion is making the information from the passage clear to everyone. Here are some ways to politely ask for more information.

- Could you explain what you meant by that?
- I'm sorry, I don't think I understood you. Would you say that another way?
- Can you tell us where you found that information?
- How did you come to feel that way?

To help everyone understand the discussion, add to what others say. Maybe you can explain an idea more clearly or give an extra bit of information. After another person has answered, take your turn. You might say, "May I add something to what you just said?" Build the discussion on what has already been talked about.

TIP 4: Use words that fit the discussion.

As you learned in Lesson 13, words can be formal or informal. Formal words are businesslike. They are grown-up and more serious. They show that you know what you're talking about and are thinking carefully. Informal words are the ones you use at home or with friends. They show that you are relaxed or comfortable.

In a small group discussion, you should stick mostly to formal language. It will help your group to think carefully about the topic. It will show others that you are taking the discussion seriously.

This doesn't mean you need to be stuffy or show off. Formal words are not always the same as fancy words. They are simply the words that smart people like you use to help each other learn.

TIP 5: Let others' ideas add to your understanding.

One reason to have a discussion is to get other people's views. If you ignore their ideas, then you aren't learning anything. You can't know everything about a subject. Think about what other group members have to say. They might have noticed something you didn't.

Even when you disagree with others, their opinions are helpful. You must think your own ideas through to understand why you disagree.

With luck, each member of the group will add to the others' knowledge. And each member of the group will learn from everyone else.

TIP 6: Present facts and opinions based on what others have said.

It is not enough to simply take a turn voicing your opinion. The point of a discussion is to make you think about a topic after each person has been heard.

Once you have listened to everyone else, think about other facts you want to bring up. Perhaps your opinion has changed based on someone else's comments. Maybe you thought of something new. If a group member has gotten some details wrong, explain what he or she missed.

Listening, thinking, and speaking again will make you a valuable member of the group.

TIP 7: Follow the rules, and carry out your assigned role.

You already know not to interrupt when another person is talking. There are other rules for making a discussion go smoothly. Here are a few, and your teacher may have others.

- Listen to each person with respect. Wait your turn.

- If you disagree, be polite. Do not argue or make fun.

- Stay on topic. Discuss the subject, not your plans for after school.

- If a group leader has been chosen, accept that person's decisions. If you are the group leader, keep the discussion on track. When everyone has talked about an idea, move on to the next. Keep an eye on the clock, and try to make sure your group discusses the whole subject before time runs out.

CCSs: SL.4.1b, SL.4.1d

- If you are asked to take notes, write down what each person says. You don't need to write every word, but get the major ideas. This is a good time to paraphrase.

TIP 8: Summarize the key ideas of the discussion.

When the discussion is over, take a moment to sum it up. Write a few notes reviewing what was said. Include ideas from all members of the group, even if you disagree with some of them. Ideas that people disagree about are often important.

Plus, you should be able to explain to others what your group talked about. If you can't remember what was said, you won't get much out of it. Writing a short summary of the discussion makes it much easier to remember. Reading your summary later can remind you, as well.

What's Your Role?

There are a number of roles you may be assigned in a reading discussion group. Each role is fun in its own way. Some of the roles you may be asked to play are listed here.

- The **discussion director** leads the conversation. He or she asks questions and encourages participation.

- The **passage picker** chooses a part of the passage for the group to read and discuss.

- The **word wizard** records definitions of unfamiliar vocabulary from the reading.

- The **investigator and connector** makes connections between the text and what he or she knows from experience or from reading other texts on the topic.

- The **illustrator** draws a picture of an important part of the text.

- The **recorder** takes notes and records the group's ideas, questions, and responses.

- The **presenter** reports the group's findings, discussions, or summary to the class.

- The **timekeeper** watches the clock, making sure the group is on task and will finish in time.

Lesson Practice begins on the following page.

Directions: This passage is about using calculators on tests. Read the passage. Then answer Numbers 1 and 2.

Calculators

The student council has asked the principal to let students use calculators during math tests. The principal has not decided yet. Students and teachers will meet to discuss the decision.

Here is what the student council says about using calculators:

- It gives children time to understand math ideas instead of working out answers.

- It helps students feel better about their math skills.

- A national group of math teachers says students should use calculators at all times. Students should spend less time working on paper.

Some of the teachers disagree. Here is what they say:

- Students do not learn basic facts without doing the work. They also have a hard time learning later skills.

- When students have to do basic math without a calculator, they can't. These students may have a hard time using money.

- Working on paper helps students learn math ideas. It trains the mind to solve problems step by step.

1. Do you agree with the student council or with the teachers about using calculators on math tests? Why?

    _____

    _____

2. Why do you think it may be good to use calculators on math tests? Why might it be bad?

    _____

    _____

Discussions

Your teacher will place you in a small group. Discuss the passage topic with your group and the answers you gave for Numbers 1 and 2. Take turns sharing your responses and listening to the responses of others.

When you are finished with your discussion, answer the questions below as a group. One group member will present your group's responses to the class.

Discussion Checklist

✔ **Members of a good discussion group:**

☐ come to the group prepared to speak about the topic

☐ share other knowledge they have about the topic

☐ ask and answer questions about the topic

☐ follow the rules for a good discussion, carry out their role, and are respectful

☐ listen to and build on the remarks of others

☐ carry out their assigned role

☐ keep to the topic of discussion

Practice

1. Did everyone in your group share the same opinion? Explain.

    _____

    _____

    _____

    _____

2. What were the best reasons given for the different views on using calculators on tests?

    _____

    _____

    _____

    _____

CCS: SL.4.4

Lesson 25: Speaking

Writing a speech is much like any other kind of writing. You must decide on a topic, support your ideas with details, and put your ideas in order. You must present your ideas clearly. The main difference is that, in the end, you must speak in front of an audience.

For many people, public speaking can be scary. They get nervous. They worry they will forget something. They think others will laugh at them. But you don't need to be scared. Instead, be prepared.

Once you have put your ideas into words, you can relax. You've already done the hard part. Reading your words to others is almost like showing off the good work you've done.

The tips in this lesson will help you build a solid speech you'll be proud to give.

 TIP 1: Choose a topic.

You have some freedom to decide what to talk about. You will probably be asked to make one of these types of speeches.

- **Report on a topic.** Do research and explain what you learned. Your topic may need to come from a given subject, such as animals or sports.

- **Explain something you have read.** Tell about a story or article. Explain what you learned or how you felt about it. You may be told what to read, or you may be allowed to choose.

- **Tell a made-up story.** Imagine a story with a beginning, middle, and end. The story might have to include certain details. For example, it might have to be set in a time before homes had electricity.

- **Tell a true story.** Think about an interesting event in your life. You may be asked for a story that fits a theme, such as a time you learned how to do something new.

You will most likely be given a time limit. If you must speak for only a few minutes, the topic should be narrow. You can't really cover the Civil War in three minutes. Choose a topic you can explain in the time you are given.

TIP 2: Prepare your speech.

Once you have a topic, decide what you want to say about it. Like other kinds of writing, a speech should have a main idea and details. It should present information in a way that makes sense. Here is a short reminder of the steps you should follow.

- **Decide on a main idea or theme.** Your speech should focus on one major point you want to make about the subject. You might decide on your main idea after you have done some research. Before you begin writing, though, you should know what you want to say. If you are telling a story, think about its theme. What lesson should readers draw from the story? What part of the story is true for everyone? You should be able to tell the theme in a sentence. For example, "True friends are there for you in good times and bad."

- **Gather details to support your ideas.** You may get information from books, Web sites, and other resources. Support main ideas in your speech with facts. Some topics may not seem to need much research. For example, a story about yourself is made up of your memories. You should still make a list of details you want to include.

- **Put your ideas in order.** When you give a speech, you only give it once. So it is important to make your ideas clear. Do you want to show how two things are alike and different? Do you want to tell about events in order? Think about the best way of presenting your ideas. If you are listing facts about an animal, don't jump from one to another. Group the details that go together. For example, size, shape, and color all tell about appearance.

- **Use an outline or note cards.** Giving a speech is not the same as reading a paper aloud. You should plan what you want to say, but don't read every word. An outline should contain the ideas and details you want to include in the order you chose. You can use the outline to remind yourself what to say. You might choose to split your outline into pieces. The pieces then go on note cards. Each note card should have one major idea and its supporting details.

TIP 3: Choose pictures, graphics, or recordings.

An old saying goes, "A picture is worth a thousand words." Sights and sounds can sometimes explain your ideas in ways that words can't. You can make your speech more interesting by adding to what the audience sees or hears. In addition to facts, you can support your main idea with photos, sound recordings, or videos.

CCSs: SL.4.4, SL.4.5

Here are a few examples of ways to add these sources to your speech.

- A **graph** might help you show the growth of your town's population over the years.

- **Paintings** would help you talk about an artist's style.

- A **sound recording** of a president's speech could help you tell why the nation went to war.

- A **photo** from a family vacation could help listeners imagine a story from your life.

- A **video** could show the best way of casting a fishing line.

Do not depend too much on these sources. Choose them carefully. Make sure they support what you plan to say. Don't let pictures or recordings take attention away from your words.

After you find a source, you must figure out how to present it. Will you need a CD player or a computer? Can you hold up a picture, or will it be too small to see? Practice using your source a few times. Don't stop your speech in its tracks to get a CD to play.

TIP 4: Speak clearly.

This might seem to go without saying, but good planning fails when you mumble or talk too fast. Speak loudly enough to be heard in the back of the room. Speak slowly enough that your words don't run together.

The main reason people speak too quietly or quickly is because they are nervous. If you are well prepared, you don't need to worry. Everyone in your audience knows what it feels like to give a speech. Most of them will be patient. If you make a few mistakes, they will understand.

If you do get anxious while speaking, here are a few ways to calm down.

- Drink a little water. This should keep your mouth from getting dry.

- Take a deep breath, and let it out slowly.

- Look for a few friendly faces, and talk mostly to them.

- Don't worry about being worried. Being a little nervous can give you energy, which can make your speech more interesting.

It is okay to glance at your notes to remember what comes next. Just remember, they are not your whole speech. Don't bury your face in your notes. Look mostly at your listeners and talk to them.

Last but not least, practice. The more times you practice your speech, even in a mirror, the better you will do.

TIP 5: Know your audience.

Just as you do when writing, you should match your speech to your audience. Are they mostly adults or children? Strangers or friends? Use your speech to show your audience how smart and prepared you are.

An important speech for a large group should be formal. **Formal** means speaking like an adult, using good grammar. It doesn't mean you should be boring or stuffy. You can be funny and interesting in a formal speech. But words like *ain't* should not be used. Instead of *buddies*, for example, say *friends*. You will probably notice which kinds of words to avoid when you practice your speech.

In each of the following sentences, replace the underlined words with more formal English.

1. When I finally got to school, I <u>was like</u>, "Sorry I'm late, Mrs. Brown."

    _____

2. Lorenzo caught the ball and started <u>booking</u> toward the end zone.

    _____

3. <u>Check out</u> this <u>cool</u> painting from Picasso's blue period.

    _____

4. <u>Me and Sheri</u> are here to teach you all about ninjas.

    _____

5. President Lincoln's speech at Gettysburg was <u>off the hook</u>.

    _____

A speech made to a small group can be more relaxed. You should still take care to make yourself understood. But your words can be friendlier and less businesslike.

Lesson Practice begins on the following page.

Directions: This passage is about the moon. Read the passage. Then respond to the prompt.

The Moon

by Colin Thorpe

The moon is our nearest neighbor. Even so, there is more to the moon than meets the eye. In fact, some things about the moon might surprise you.

Do you know where moonlight comes from? The moon shines brightly in the night sky, but it has no light of its own. Instead, the moon reflects light from the sun.

When you shine a flashlight on a wall in a dark room, you see a bright spot on the wall. When sunlight hits the moon, the moon glows brightly, too. We can see the moon only when sunlight shines on the part that faces us.

The moon may seem to be brighter than the stars, but it isn't. Like our sun, stars make their own light. The moon looks brighter only because it is closer to us. The stars seem dimmer because they are so far away.

If you were to hop on a rocket and travel to the moon, you would find things there to be very different from Earth. For starters, there's no life on the moon. There's no air, no wind, and only very tiny amounts of frozen water. Like Earth, the moon has mountains and valleys. But it has no rivers, lakes, or oceans. Also, there is no weather. That means there are no cloudy, windy, or rainy days. And the sky is always black, day or night.

A day on the moon lasts 15 Earth days, and so does a night! In the sunlight, the temperature on the moon gets hot enough to boil water. In the darkness, the temperature can drop to 250° below zero. When astronauts visited the moon between 1969 and 1972, they had to wear space suits to protect themselves from the heat and the cold. Any future visitors will have to wear them, too.

If you were on the moon, you could not hear a fellow astronaut talking unless you used a radio. There is no air to carry the sound of your voice. Also, you weigh more on Earth than you would weigh on the moon. This is because the gravity on the moon is much weaker than the gravity on Earth.

Someday, people may build space stations on the moon. Then they could live there safely. They could grow plants and raise animals. Telescopes placed on the moon could be used to see farther into space than telescopes on Earth can see. And rockets could travel to other planets from the moon more easily than they can from Earth.

By the time you grow up, you may be able to travel to the moon. If you do go, don't forget your camera. There's a great view of a beautiful planet called Earth.

Speaking

Plan a speech in which you explain the differences between the moon and Earth.

Directions: Write notes for your speech in the space below.

Using your notes on the previous page, you will present your speech to your class. Your teacher will give you specific instructions for your presentation.

Speaker's Checklist

✓ **I write and present my best speech when:**

☐ I report on a topic, explain a text, or tell a story in an organized way

☐ I use facts and details to support a main idea and theme

☐ I include pictures, graphics, or recordings to support my ideas

☐ I speak clearly and loudly enough to be heard and understood

☐ I speak at an understandable pace

☐ I use formal English when presenting to a large group or adult audience

Mechanics Toolbox

Mechanics Toolbox

 Subject-Verb Agreement

The **subject** tells who or what a sentence is about. The **verb** tells what the subject does. Some subjects are singular. Other subjects are plural.

Examples:

The sun shines.

The dogs bark.

The sun is a singular subject. There is just one sun. *The dogs* is a plural subject. There is more than one dog. The verbs *shines* and *bark* tell what each subject does.

A subject and verb need to match in number, or **agree**.

Examples:

Franklin runs up the hill. (correct)

The little boy run to catch up with his big sister. (incorrect)

The plural verb, *run*, does not agree with the singular subject, *The little boy*. The correct sentence is:

The little boy runs to catch up with his big sister.

Pronoun-Antecedent Agreement

A **pronoun** is a word that takes the place of a noun. An **antecedent** is the word that a pronoun replaces.

Example:

The ducklings followed their mother in a line along the shore. Then they plopped into the lake after her.

In the second sentence, the words *they* and *her* are pronouns. The antecedent of *they* is the plural noun *ducklings*. The antecedent of *her* is the singular noun *mother*.

Pronouns and antecedents need to agree. If the antecedent is more than one, the pronoun needs to show more than one. If the antecedent is male, female, or neither, the pronoun also needs to be male, female, or neither.

Examples:

Geoff read another chapter of the mystery before he went to bed. (correct)

Jessica and Stacey walked to the park. She had a picnic there. (incorrect)

The singular pronoun, *She*, does not agree with the antecedent. *Jessica and Stacey* is more than one. It needs a plural pronoun. The correct sentence is:

Jessica and Stacey walked to the park. They had a picnic there.

 ## Words for Effect

Good writing uses vivid words. Compare these examples:

The girls <u>went happily</u> across the lawn. (weak word choices)

The girls <u>skipped</u> and <u>giggled</u> across the lawn. (strong word choices)

The words *skipped* and *giggled* are strong and vivid. They help the reader "see" the girls.

Using more words is not always better. Vivid words can say a lot on their own. Compare these examples:

The crowd <u>made a lot of noise</u>. (weak word choices)

The crowd <u>roared</u>. (strong word choice)

Adjectives and Adverbs

An **adjective** tells more about a noun. The underlined words in these sentences are adjectives.

Jasmine's bicycle is <u>blue</u>.

Artie ate his <u>favorite</u> meal of spaghetti and meatballs.

The adjective *blue* tells more about the noun *bicycle*. It tells about the color of the bicycle. The adjective *favorite* tells more about the noun *meal*. It tells that the meal is the one Artie likes best.

An **adverb** tells more about a verb, adjective, or another adverb. It answers the question *How?* The underlined words in these sentences are adverbs.

The cat slinked <u>quietly</u> out of the room.

We were happy to go swimming on that <u>very</u> hot Saturday.

The adverb *quietly* tells how the cat slinked. The adverb *very* tells how hot that Saturday was.

Mechanics Toolbox

 **Complete Sentences**

A sentence tells a complete thought. It has a subject and a verb.

Example:

We laughed.

This sentence is short, but it is complete. It has a subject, *We*. The verb, *laughed*, tells what the subject does.

Some sentences tell two or more complete thoughts. Words like *and*, *but*, and *or* are used to connect the thoughts. In the following sentence, the complete thoughts are underlined.

Dark clouds covered the sky, and rain began to fall.

In other sentences, a less important idea is added to a complete thought. Words like *when*, *because*, *if*, and *after* are used to connect the less important idea to the main thought. In the following sentences, the less important idea is underlined once and the main thought is underlined twice.

My father wakes up when the birds begin to sing.

Because he leaves for work so early, my father also comes home early.

A **run-on sentence** tells two or more thoughts without using any connecting words.

Example:

The sirens grew louder and louder, the fire trucks rushed down the avenue.

You can correct a run-on sentence by splitting it into two complete sentences. You can also correct it by adding a connecting word.

Examples:

The sirens grew louder and louder. The fire trucks rushed down the avenue.

The sirens grew louder and louder, <u>and</u> the fire trucks rushed down the avenue.

A **sentence fragment** does not tell a complete thought.

Example:

The panda that was just born at the zoo.

The subject, *The panda*, does not have a verb. You can correct a sentence fragment by completing the thought. The fragment is completed by adding a verb.

Example:

The panda that was just born at the zoo <u>is</u> still too young for visitors to see.

298

Mechanics Toolbox

Confused Words

Homophones are two or more words that sound alike but are spelled differently and mean different things. They are easy to confuse. Here are some homophones.

Homophones and Meanings	Examples
A lot: many **Allot:** to give out	Janice used <u>a lot</u> of fruit to make a big salad for the party. We will <u>allot</u> five cards to each player.
Board: a plank **Bored:** uninterested, dull	We need just one more <u>board</u> to complete our tree house. On the second day of the car trip, Terrence was <u>bored</u>.
Hear: to take in sounds **Here:** at this place	We could <u>hear</u> the children shouting before we saw them. We keep a spare key <u>here</u>, under this rock.
It's: it is **Its:** belonging to it	<u>It's</u> not likely to snow in June. The garden is famous for <u>its</u> prize-winning roses.
Knew: past tense of *know* **New:** opposite of *old*	Johnny <u>knew</u> the name of every student at his school. Angela wore her <u>new</u> bracelet the day after her birthday.
Their: belonging to them **There:** at that place **They're:** they are	<u>Their</u> house has a big porch, whereas ours has none. If you go <u>there</u> to visit, they will ask you to stay for lunch. <u>They're</u> friendly and enjoy company.
Weak: Opposite of *strong* **Week:** A series of seven days	The baby birds were still too <u>weak</u> to fly. In one more <u>week</u> our vacation will begin.

Mechanics Toolbox

Other words are also commonly confused. Some of them are nearly homophones. Some of them are similar in both sound and meaning. Here are some examples.

Commonly Confused Words and Meanings	Examples
Accept: to agree **Except:** not including	I hope that you <u>accept</u> our invitation to play in the recital! Everyone had fun at the game <u>except</u> for Russell, who was too tired.
Affect: to cause a change **Effect:** result	I cried, but the end of the movie did not <u>affect</u> my mother. The floods were not the only <u>effect</u> of the heavy rains.
Close: to shut **Clothes:** garments, such as a shirt or pants	Mrs. Lee asked me to <u>close</u> the door behind me. I wore my best <u>clothes</u> to the wedding, including the red tie my grandfather gave me.
Loose: opposite of *tight* **Lose:** opposite of *win*	My shoelaces were <u>loose</u>, and I almost tripped on them. It never feels good to <u>lose</u>.
Than: in comparison with **Then:** at that time	My sister likes playing soccer much more <u>than</u> I do. We did not know as much <u>then</u> as we do now.
Weather: the state of the atmosphere in a place **Whether:** shows a choice	The <u>weather</u> here changes quickly, from sunshine to snow in moments. <u>Whether</u> or not you come with me, I am going swimming.

The verbs *lie* and *lay* are also commonly confused. Their meanings are similar. Also, the past tense of *lie* is *lay*. However, *lie* never has an object. *Lay* always has an object. Here are some examples.

Lie: to rest, recline **Lay:** past tense of *lie*	Go <u>lie</u> on the bed until you feel better. Thomas <u>lay</u> there until dinner was ready.
Lay: to put down **Laid:** past tense of *lay*	I <u>lay</u> the flowers on the table. Irma <u>laid</u> the tools she needed on the counter.

 ## Word Choice

Good writing uses exact words. Compare these examples:

The boy was <u>tired</u>.

The boy was <u>sleepy</u>.

The boy was <u>worn out</u>.

Sleepy and *tired* have similar meanings. The word *sleepy* gives more information than the word *tired*. It tells the way the boy is tired: he needs sleep. The word *sleepy* is a more exact word than *tired*.

Worn out and *tired* also have similar meanings. *Worn out* is also more exact than *tired*. It tells that the boy is tired from playing or working hard.

Like vivid words, exact words can say a lot on their own. Compare these examples:

The class <u>had a good time</u> at the farm. (weak word choice)

The class <u>enjoyed</u> the farm. (strong word choice)

Mechanics Toolbox

Here are some weak words and some stronger words you can use in their place.

Weak Words	Strong Words
Cold	• chilly • frozen • wintery
Warm	• boiling • burning • tropical
Big	• huge • giant • vast
Small	• puny • slight • tiny
Happy	• delighted • pleased • thrilled
Sad	• depressed • gloomy • miserable

Mechanics Toolbox

Punctuation

Every sentence ends with a punctuation mark. A sentence that tells a statement ends with a **period (.).** For example:

> We go to the farmers' market on Saturday mornings.

A sentence that gives a command also ends with a period. For example:

> Please get me a pound of apples when you are there.

A sentence that asks a question ends with a **question mark (?).** For example:

> Does anyone sell fresh eggs at the market?

A sentence that shows excitement ends with an **exclamation point (!).** For example:

> That pumpkin weighs 300 pounds!

A **quotation** shows the exact words that someone said. A quotation begins and ends with **quotation marks (" ").** For example:

> Rami said, "Those cider doughnuts are the best."

Notice that a **comma (,)** is used before the quotation. In the following example, a comma is used at the end of the quotation.

> "I like the doughnuts from our bakery better," Allison said.

If the quotation asks a question, a question mark is used. If the quotation shows excitement, an exclamation point is used.

> Examples:
>
> "Is the market also open on Wednesdays?" Rami asked.
>
> "I wish it were open every day!" Allison exclaimed.

Mechanics Toolbox